THE
EASTER
BOOK

ANNE FARNCOMBE

NATIONAL CHRISTIAN EDUCATION COUNCIL
Robert Denholm House
Nutfield, Redhill, Surrey, RH1 4HW

TO VAL

A companion volume, THE CHRISTMAS BOOK,
also by Anne Farncombe, is available from NCEC

Biblical quotations are from the Good News Bible, © 1976 American Bible Society,
New York.

First published 1984
© 1983 Anne Farncombe

ISBN 0-7197-0386-7

Typeset by Solo Typesetting, Maidstone, Kent
Printed and bound by Mackays of Chatham

CONTENTS

THE STORY OF EASTER

When we think about Easter, and the biblical accounts of it, perhaps the first words that come into our minds are 'HE IS RISEN!'

They are words that Christians all round the world say to each other on Easter Day. And yet, in the Gospels of Matthew, Mark, Luke and John, the story of the 'rising' or 'resurrection' of Jesus is written about and remembered in many different ways. Perhaps this story will help you to understand why:

Suppose for a moment you have a brother — let's call him Kevin — and that he has a birthday on 5 July. When he grows up, Kevin somehow becomes famous and well-known, and you are asked to write a book about his early life, with the help of the rest of your family.

'Do you remember, when he was about eight, Kevin had a bike for his birthday?' you ask your parents.

'I remember it well,' says Dad. 'We had to hide it in the coal-shed for a week beforehand so that he wouldn't see it until the fifth.'

'Yes, he was eight all right that birthday,' says Mother. 'And wasn't he thrilled with the bike? He wanted to cycle to school that morning, before he'd even learnt to ride it!'

'Wasn't that the day that awful boy Jack something came to his birthday tea?' your sister Pamela remembers. 'Kevin blew out his candles, then that boy upset his glass of orange all over the cake!'

'Oh, I think it only went over the plate,' says Mother, thinking back.

'And then Kevin chased Jack into the garden!' says your younger brother Martin.

'How do you know?' asks Pamela. 'You weren't even born then!'

'We've told him about it often enough,' laughs Mother.

'I don't remember what happened afterwards,' says Dad. 'I just know we were left to clean up everything!'

The family were remembering a special day — a birthday. If they had been asked to remember what happened on, say 29 January that year, they may not have been able to remember so much, or had so much to say. But, as it was a celebration day, they remembered, just as we can all bring back the memory of special days in our lives, or in the lives of our best friends. Did you notice, too, how the younger brother, who hadn't even been there at the time, added something that he had been told about?

On that first Easter Day something very special happened, something unexpected and startling. No wonder everyone remembered it!

The story of what had happened was talked about, described, thought over and finally — many, many years later — written about.

It is not surprising that each person writing about it put something different.

Some of the writers had never met Jesus, and were writing about what they had been told.

But one thing was important to all of them — the fact that Jesus, having died and been buried, had come alive again.

He was recognised, he spoke, he walked, he ate.

Had the disciples seen a ghost, a hallucination? But many of them were down-to-earth, ordinary fishermen! Had they dreamed it up because they were expecting it to happen? But they were not expecting it, they had seen him die; the women had gone to the tomb with spices to anoint a dead body; none thought they would ever see him again, alive.

Now look in your Bible and read the different accounts of that special day:

Matthew 28.1-10
Mark 16.1-8
Luke 24.1-12
John 20.1-10

Further on in the Bible we can read Simon Peter's own words about it:

Acts 3.15

You killed the one who leads to life, but God raised him from death - and we are witnesses to this.

Later on that same day, when rumours began about a risen Lord, two of the followers of Jesus were walking back to Emmaus, a village about 11km away from Jerusalem. They could talk about only one thing — the events of the past few days.

Deep in their discussion, a third person caught up with them, and began to join in their conversation . . .

Read what happened on this walk; it is one of the most vivid accounts in the New Testament: Luke 24.13-35.

It was like a fire burning in us when he talked with us on the road!

The two friends of Jesus tried to explain to the disciples what had happened on the road to Emmaus. The disciples were meeting in secret, if the Jewish authorities knew where they were they, too, would probably have been arrested and thrown into prison, or even executed, simply for being the friends and followers of Jesus.

. . . they stopped talking, and shrank back.

What had stunned them and made them terrified?

We are told the friends of Jesus were 'full of joy and wonder'.

Let us now go back to remember what had led up to this wonderful happening.

The week had begun in triumph . . .

HOSANNA!

Jesus and his little band of followers had travelled down from Galilee to Jerusalem to be there in time for the Passover Festival.

Jesus knew he was in danger of arrest, even execution, if he showed himself in the city, and his disciples were afraid.

The Passover is an important festival for us. Every year at this time we remember how Moses led our people out of slavery in Egypt, long ago

But Jesus had to show them that his triumph would only come after he had suffered and died. This was God's plan, and the only way.

Jesus told his disciples what he wanted them to do:

Go to that village where you'll find a donkey and her colt

Bring them to me

But...

Just tell anyone who asks that the Master needs them

Read what happened next, in Matthew 21.6-11.

NOW Pretend you were someone in that crowd of people, determined to follow Jesus to see where he went. Write up your diary for that day, describing the kingly ride into Jerusalem.

OR

Imagine that you were a reporter for a local newspaper, sent to write about this procession, or 'demonstration'. How would you give your readers a clear picture of what was happening? Make drawings, in place of photographs, for the newspaper.

OR

If you have a tape-recorder, and a few friends to help you, produce a radio report about the entry of Jesus into Jerusalem. Record 'interviews' with a person in the crowd, one of Jesus' disciples, and a Pharisee who had watched the proceedings and who hoped Jesus would be arrested before the Festival.

TROUBLE!

Maybe the people in the crowd that day did not realise what Jesus was doing; but the Jewish people in authority knew their Scriptures very well:

Zechariah

Your King is coming to you! He comes triumphant and victorious, but humble and riding on a donkey

Zechariah 9.9

That is how our Messiah will come! This Jesus is telling us HE is the Messiah! We must stop this nonsense!

But it calls for caution.... He has the people on his side at the moment

NOW LOOK WHAT HE'S UP TO!

Read Matthew 21.12-16 to find out what had upset them now

Where did Jesus spend the night? (Read verse 17.) He probably stayed at the home of his friends, Martha and Mary and their brother Lazarus.

The Jewish authorities had become very angry, but how could they arrest Jesus without causing an uproar among the crowds in Jerusalem? And what charge could they bring against him?

He spent each night in a village outside the city, and during the day he was surrounded by his 'supporters' inside the walls of Jerusalem. Somehow they had to avoid a major riot, with the city so full of people ready to celebrate the Passover Festival.

Then came the break they were looking for:

Jesus, knowing about Judas' secret plot with the chief priests, arranged to hold his last meal with his friends, the disciples. It had to take place secretly, under cover of darkness.

What was the secret sign which Jesus said would lead them to the house where the supper was to be held?

THE LAST SUPPER

That night Jesus and his disciples met in the secret room. Jesus wanted to make quite sure that his friends understood that his way of conquering was through love and service. He chose to do this by an action, very simple, and yet with so much meaning.

 What did he do? Read John 13.3-5.

Afterwards Jesus sat down at the table again and asked his friends if they had understood why he had done this. Perhaps some of them had looked bewildered; Peter had even spoken out against Jesus' action. So Jesus went on to explain it to them: read John 13.15-17.

Now they were ready to eat the meal together. During the meal Judas slipped out to tell the chief priests where they could find Jesus later that evening.

The last supper itself is a meal that Christians everywhere act out again and again, reminding themselves of this last moment of fellowship that Jesus had with his friends. This special service has several names, including the Sacrament of Holy Communion, the Mass, the Eucharist.

Jesus took a piece of  , gave thanks for it, then broke it.

What did he say as he did this? Read Luke 22.19.

Then he took a of wine, gave thanks again, and passed it round.

Read his words about this action, in Luke 22.20.

16

Jesus then told his disciples to remember and obey a new rule, or commandment, he was giving them.

Love one another. As I have loved you, so you must love one another

John 13.34

He also said that people would learn something if his friends obeyed this rule.

What was it? Find out by reading John 13.35.

Now the time had come when Jesus knew he would have to be particularly brave. It meant leaving that safe, secret room and walking across the deep valley and up into the Garden of Gethsemane. This was a garden set apart on the slope of the Mount of Olives. His friends followed, afraid, and yet not realising quite how imminent was the danger for all of them.

They had often met in the garden before; Judas Iscariot knew that in this lonely place the guards sent by the chief priests could find Jesus and arrest him with little disturbance.

In the garden, Jesus spent his time in prayer. The disciples, worn out, fell asleep.

Read about the moment of arrest, and try to imagine being there — seeing the flaming torches getting nearer, and hearing the voices and hurrying footsteps: Mark 14.32-46.

What did the disciples do? Read the answer in Mark 14.50.

ON TRIAL

The secret meal and the arrest of Jesus happened on the Thursday night, and the Jewish rulers realised they must get the trial over, and sentence passed, before the Sabbath, which began at 6 o'clock on Friday evening. During the night, Jesus was taken to the High Priest.

Peter followed, but under cover of darkness. In the High Priest's courtyard the servants thought they recognised Peter, and challenged him. Three times Peter denied all knowledge of his Master: 'I don't even know the man!' he said.

The supreme Jewish court of law was called together hurriedly. 'He must be sent to Pilate straight away!' it decided.

Pontius Pilate was the Roman governor stationed in Jerusalem. At Passover time he had to make sure that no politically motivated pilgrims caused any trouble. He did not really want to be involved in a Jewish religious dispute.

The Jewish lawyers were clever. They had to make the charges against Jesus valid in Roman law, too.

Prisoner: *Jesus, son of Joseph*

Charges:

1   Behaviour likely to cause a breach of the peace. Agitation of the crowds.

2   Treason against Rome. The prisoner has been heard to discourage people from paying taxes to Rome.

3   Self-nomination as King of the Jews.

Jesus was taken to appear before Pilate:

Herod was pleased to have the chance to see this man Jesus. He had heard he could perform miracles, but was most disappointed in him. Jesus would not even speak, which made Herod very angry.

DEATH SENTENCE

Pilate still did not want responsibility for the death of Jesus, and did not think the case against him was strong enough. Again he tried to save him.

At Passover time it was the custom for the Roman authorities to set free one prisoner. Surely, thought Pilate, the people who had welcomed Jesus as a king only a few days earlier would cry for his release now.

But I was wrong!

Who did the crowd, encouraged by the Jewish chief priests and lawyers, ask to have freed?

Read all about this mob frenzy, in Luke 23.18-23.

And so Pilate passed the death sentence on Jesus.

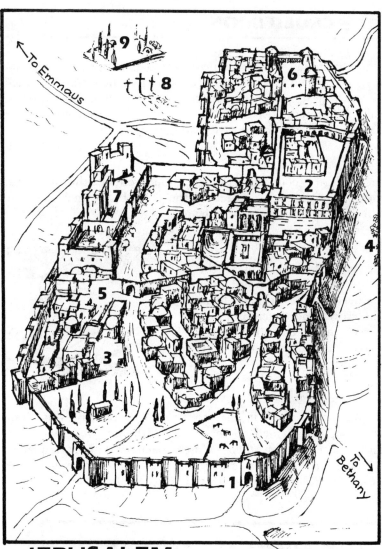

JERUSALEM

Key

1 Gate into Jerusalem
2 The Temple
3 The last supper was held in a house like one of these
4 The Mount of Olives
5 The High Priest lived within the walls of Jerusalem
6 The Antonia Fortress, where Jesus was interviewed by Pilate
7 Herod's Palace
8 Golgotha
9 Site of the tomb

21

THE CRUCIFIXION

To be crucified was a terrible way to die. Jesus was beaten, and then compelled to carry the cross on which he would be nailed, all the way to his place of execution. By this time he was physically exhausted; he had had no sleep the previous night, and had already been tormented by Herod's soldiers.

The place of execution was a rocky mound outside the city walls, known as Golgotha — place of the skull. It is sometimes now called by its Latin name of Calvary.

Crowds of people lined the route. At one point the soldiers picked a man from the crowd and ordered him to carry the cross that Jesus could no longer manage to drag along.

It was nine o'clock in the morning of the Friday when Jesus was crucified, nailed to his cross. With him were two other men, criminals, on their crosses. Each cross bore a placard telling people for what crime each man had been sentenced to death. Over the head of Jesus the notice read:

THE KING OF THE JEWS

This did not please the chief priests, of course, but Pilate would not alter it.

BURIAL

The crowds who had followed all the way to Golgotha stood by, jeering and laughing. But a group of women stood near, crying. Mary, the mother of Jesus, was one of the group; perhaps she heard his whispered words as he hung there.

Read what Jesus said: Luke 23.34.

At three o'clock that afternoon Jesus died.

A member of the Jewish Council, a man called Joseph of Arimathea, came forward at once to ask Pilate for the body of Jesus. Joseph was a secret admirer of the teacher and healer, and was anxious to take his body for burial in a rock-tomb he owned.

These tombs were the normal burial places for the dead. They were caves cut out of the rock, with a stone slab inside on which the body was placed. To prevent any kind of disturbance a heavy, wheel-shaped stone lay in a groove in the ground outside the cave, waiting to be rolled across the entrance, to close it.

The body of Jesus was taken down from the cross, wrapped in white linen, and taken to the tomb. The stone was rolled into position.

It was Friday, late afternoon, and the Sabbath day was about to begin. The women would have to wait until the Sunday morning before they could take spices to anoint the body . . .

Now read again the story of Easter as it is recorded in John 20.1,11-29.

Some of the disciples returned to Galilee after the Passover week in Jerusalem. They were tired both physically and emotionally, and yet felt a great weight had been lifted from them. Their despair and grief had turned into an overwhelming joy when they had seen for themselves that their leader and master, their Lord, was not dead.

By the Lake of Galilee Jesus met them again early one morning, and shared breakfast with them. Read the account of this in John 21.1-14.

Later that morning, Jesus took Simon Peter aside. 'Take care of my sheep,' he said, when he had made sure that Peter was quite ready to be loyal and loving again.

'You will be given power,' Jesus told his friends. 'Strength for all you have to do for me.'

On a lonely hillside in Galilee, with the countryside spreading out below and around them, Jesus gave his friends one last command.

What was this command?
Read Matthew 28.19-20.

It was now up to them, this small band of followers, to spread the Good News of Jesus far and wide.

EASTER BEGINS

Easter is a time of sadness and gladness for Christians. It is a time for remembering the death of Jesus, and a time for rejoicing that he rose again.

Easter really begins seven weeks before Easter Sunday, usually in February, with the period called Lent. Hundreds of years ago the Christian Church decided that people should spend a time being solemn and fasting. They should, said the priests, remember the forty days Jesus spent fasting in the wilderness, and spend much time in prayer and refusing to eat many of the foods that they usually enjoyed.

So, as Lent began on a Wednesday — Ash Wednesday — the previous day was spent as a holiday, for sport and feasting, in readiness for the solemn weeks ahead.

Some of the games and sports played were ones of sheer brute force, covering long distances before the winners were decided.

All 'luxury' food left in larders had to be eaten up on this day, particularly meat, butter and eggs.

The people found that eggs, when mixed with flour and milk, made filling pancakes. The pancakes, fried in butter, provided them with a good meal before the hungry time ahead.

SHROVE TUESDAY

This Tuesday of feasting before Lent was known as Shrove Tuesday because the people were first called to church to be SHRIVEN, or SHRIVED, which means to be forgiven for all the sins they confessed.

Today most of us cling to the practice of eating pancakes on Shrove Tuesday, perhaps without much idea of why or when the custom began. We also know that the pancakes should be tossed during cooking, and that nowadays they are usually eaten with lemon juice and sugar.

Strange old customs connected with Shrove Tuesday still remain in many parts of the country.

In Olney, Buckinghamshire, housewives are still invited to take part in a pancake race from the Market Square to the Parish Church. You may have seen it filmed on television. An old story tells how the custom began in 1445:

In memory of this happening the pancake race is held each year. The ladies line up in the Market Square in the morning, wearing head scarves and aprons, and carrying a cooked pancake in a frying pan. As the competitors run to the church, a distance of over 350m (400 yards), they have to toss the pancakes. The winner receives a kiss and a prayer book from the vicar who says to her, 'The peace of the Lord be always with you.'

Later, all the ladies go into the church, prop their frying pans against the altar, and take part in a service.

Over thirty years ago, the people in the town of Liberal, in Kansas, USA, began to take a particular interest in the Olney race. They now hold their own pancake race, phoning the town in England afterwards to compare winners' times and performance.

Many other ancient Shrove-tide customs are still carried on, the most common being the ringing of the 'pancake bell' on Shrove Tuesday morning.

At Westminster School, in London, however, there is held what is known as a Pancake Greaze every year on Shrove Tuesday. No one knows exactly how old this 'sport' is, but it probably began in the Middle Ages.

In the days when the school began, all the boys were taught in one very large hall. A curtain hanging from a long iron pole divided the older boys from the younger ones.

On Shrove Tuesday, the curtain was drawn aside, and the school cook arrived, carrying a pancake in a frying pan. It was his job to toss the pancake over the iron rod. When he did so, all the boys rushed forward to see who could carry away the pancake, and the winner received a guinea (£1.05) from the Dean. If the cook failed to toss the pancake over the bar, we are told that he was attacked by the boys!

The custom still goes on, with modifications. Now only one boy from each form takes part; the curtain is no longer there, although the iron rod remains. The boys are assembled, then a procession of the Dean and Headmaster, followed by the cook, enters. The cook tosses his freshly-made pancake high over the 4.8m (16ft) bar, and the boys rush for it, forming what looks like a rugger scrum! At the end of two minutes, 'Time' is called, and, in dead silence, the remains of the pancake are examined. The winner is the boy who has managed to hang on to the largest amount of pancake, and the Dean presents him with the customary guinea.

In Somerset, a much smaller school carries on another custom associated with Pancake Day. It probably began when the people, wishing to use up all their eggs quickly before the beginning of Lent, made a sport of it. It is said that the parishioners of the church presented all the broken eggs afterwards to the vicar, to last him through the meatless days of Lent.

Nowadays the custom is carried on by the children of the Primary School in Stoke St Gregory, in very much the same way as it was hundreds of years ago.

On Pancake Day each child brings to school an ordinary, uncooked, hen's egg, with his or her name written on it. All the eggs are put into a sieve which is gently shaken. As each egg cracks or breaks, it is removed, until only one remains, which is called the 'Master Egg'. This egg must then be broken, to prove that it is raw — someone might try to cheat by bringing along a hard-boiled one!

Since 1982 an annual cup, presented by a London Craft Guild, has been given to the child with the winning egg.

Along with other games and sports, skipping used to be a favourite pastime on Shrove Tuesday. Perhaps it was a good way of keeping warm in the February or early March weather!

In Scarborough, Yorkshire, this custom still survives. The Pancake Bell is rung at noon for a church service, and then at 2pm men, women and children gather near the seafront to skip.

In many Spanish-speaking countries, and in France and parts of America, Shrove-tide is a time of carnival, of processions and dancing, music and feasting. People in these mainly Roman Catholic countries are discouraged from eating meat during Lent, so Shrove Tuesday became known as MARDI GRAS, which means 'Fat Tuesday'. On this day quantities of meat are finished up.

The word carnival comes from the Latin words *carnem levare*, meaning 'put away flesh, or meat'.

One of the best known carnivals is held in the American town of New Orleans, where there is a procession of highly coloured floats, jazz bands, and riders on horseback.

Some other countries eat pancakes, as we do, on Shrove Tuesday, but many have their own traditional food on that day. A recipe for one of them is given on the next page.

Even in our own country, the people of Norwich have their own particular Shrove Tuesday buns. These are called 'Coquille buns'. Long ago they were sold in the streets by people who shouted,

> 'Hot penny coquilles,
> smoking all hot,
> smoking all hot,
> hot penny coquilles!'

On menus in restaurants you may sometimes see the word 'coquilles'. If you ordered them you would not receive buns but a plateful of fish called scallops! We can only guess that the first Norwich coquille buns were shaped like scallop shells. Sometimes they were also known as cockeals, or cookeels. Perhaps the American word 'cookies', meaning biscuits, came from this word, too.

Pancakes

4 tablespoons plain flour
2 dessertspoons sugar
2 eggs
pinch of salt
milk
butter

Put the flour, sugar and salt into a bowl and stir. Add the beaten eggs slowly, then a teaspoonful of melted butter. Stir in enough milk to make the batter like cream. Beat it well, until smooth and frothy. Put a little butter into a heated frying pan until it is really hot but not burning. Pour in about two tablespoons of the batter, spreading it around the pan. Let it cook for a minute until it is set. Now toss it, or flip it over, so that the other side can cook. Carefully fold the pancake and keep it hot.

It can be eaten with sugar and lemon juice, or with jam.

Coquille buns

200g (or 8oz) SR flour
25g (or 1oz) lard
25g (or 1oz) margarine
50g (or 2oz) sugar
½ egg
1 teaspoon mixed spice
1 cup dried fruit
milk

Rub the fats and flour together and add the sugar, fruit and spice. Mix in the egg and enough milk to make a stiff dough. Put it on a floured board and roll it out to at least 2cm (or 1in) thick. Cut into squares. Cook at 375°F (or 190°C or Gas 5) for about 20 minutes. Eat the buns hot, spread with butter in the centre.

Pretzels

1 packet dried yeast
1 cup lukewarm water
3 cups plain flour
2 teaspoons baking powder
pinch salt
1 egg

Stir the yeast and water together until the yeast dissolves, then leave to one side for 15 minutes. Put flour, baking powder and salt into a bowl, then slowly add the cup of yeast and water. Add the beaten egg, mixing it all to a dough. Add a little more flour if it is too soft. Knead the dough well on a floured board. Put it in a bowl, cover with a damp cloth, and leave in a warm place for about 30 minutes, when it will have risen. Knead it again on the floured board. Roll out fairly thinly, then cut into strips about 15cm (or 6in) long and 2cm (or ¾in) wide. Twist these strips into knots. Leave them on a board while you boil a pan of water. Put about 3 pretzels into the boiling water. They will sink, but when they come to the surface again, lift them out onto a greased baking tray. Do this with all the pretzels. Then brush them with beaten egg, and sprinkle them with sesame or poppy seeds if you wish. Bake in a hot oven (450°F, 225°C, Gas 7) for about 15 minutes.

Eat them hot or cold, with butter.

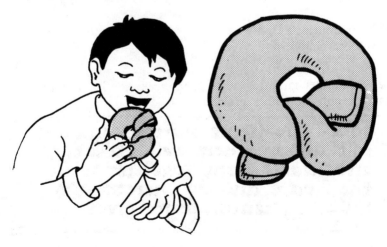

MEDIEVAL COOKS

In the 14th and 15th centuries people did not have as much choice as we do in what they could eat. Their food came from the land around them, from the animals they kept and the crops they grew. Usually the food was cooked in large kitchens with several open fires.

Many of their recipes included great quantities of eggs. This was because, in those days, the eggs were not nearly as big as ours. Nowadays commercial egg-farming has increased the size of eggs. The people also kept a lot of chickens, as they were cheap to feed, and provided good meat as well as eggs.

crocus

Cooks in medieval days also liked to colour their food brightly. Powdered saffron was added to many dishes, making everything brilliant yellow. Saffron came from a kind of crocus flower brought into Britain about five hundred years ago. It was also used as a dye and a medicine. One town which became famous for marketing the powdered plant was Walden, in Essex. It became known as Saffron Walden.

Other colourings used were obtained from spinach, parsley, and powdered sandalwood.

Can you understand this recipe for pancakes, written as it would have been in the 15th century?

> Take fayre floure, saffron, sugre and salt, and mix hem well. Take eggs and meddle hem together with the floure, and do thereto add milk. Fry hem in fayre grece.

Ask if you may invite a few friends to tea on Shrove Tuesday. You could give them pancakes, coquille buns, and pretzels to eat. The buns and pretzels could be made a few days beforehand and wrapped in foil. Both of them freeze well if you want to make them even earlier. Make sure that you have eggs and plain flour ready to make the pancakes, and lemon slices if you like to serve these on top.

You could ask your friends to bring an initialled egg each, then 'shackle' them in a sieve or colander (see page 29) before using them to make pancakes.

The pancakes need to be made just before they are eaten, so your guests should have arrived before you begin cooking the pancakes. Perhaps everyone would like a turn at tossing them!

But be careful — pancakes are not very nice scraped off the floor!

After tea, play some of the old games people used to enjoy at this time of year: marbles, or skipping, perhaps.

Spinning-tops were also very popular. They were made of turned wood, and had a pointed end. Children carried sticks with a length of string attached. The end of the string was twisted round the spinning-top, which was then held on, or near, the ground. The stick was pulled sharply so that the string came away from the top, causing it to spin rapidly on its point. Really clever children could then whip the top with the string to keep it spinning for a long time!

Make your own simple spinning top

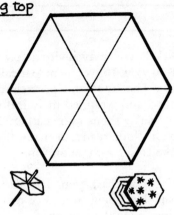

Trace this shape onto card and cut out. Colour the sections, or make your own patterns in bright colours on the shape.

Push a pointed matchstick through the centre.

Hold the top of the matchstick lightly, spin the disc, and let go.

For a party, each guest could make a top, then all spin them at once to see whose top spins the longest.

If you want to dress up for your pancake tea party, make some chef's hats, and ask each guest to bring an apron. You might be able to hold a pancake race in the garden!

To make a chef's hat:

You will need:
stiff white paper, about 25cm x 60cm (or 10in x 24in); white tissue paper about 40cm (or 16in) square; glue.

Measure round your head and add 2.5cm (or 1in) to the length. Cut the stiff paper to this length and glue the shorter ends to make a cylinder.

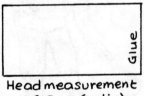

Head measurement
+2.5cm (or 1in)

Take the square of tissue paper and fold it in half diagonally. Do this twice more. You should now have a shape like this: ———▶

Cut through all thicknesses on the dotted line. Unfold the paper, which should be circular. Make cuts, about 2cm (or ¾in) all round the edge. Put glue carefully around the edge of the circle, fold back along the cuts, and stick them round the inside of the cylinder as shown. When the glue is dry, puff up the tissue paper with your hand from inside the cylinder.

WORD PUZZLE FOR SHROVE TUESDAY

The words below are all connected with Shrove Tuesday. Fit them, to read downwards, into the squares. One of them has been done for you.

BUNS	CARNIVAL	FAST	FOOD
PLAY	PANCAKES	FLOUR	TOSS
LENT	SKIP	RACE	EGG
	SHRIVEN		

ASH WEDNESDAY and LENT

For many hundreds of years Christians have spent the weeks before Easter in sorrow and self-denial. They were not only sad because the time was coming when they would particularly remember the death of Jesus, but they were ashamed when they thought of all the sins they had committed. Some people still make Lent a time to give up something they enjoy, but many now make a resolution to get something done during this period, to achieve something they have found very difficult, or to accomplish tasks that are disliked.

The word LENT comes from an old English word meaning Spring — LENGTEN — the time when the days begin to lengthen. In the 4th century, the Christian Church decided that the forty days before Easter should be spent remembering the time when Jesus went into the wilderness, or desert, and was tempted. Read about this in Luke 4.1-13. Sundays, though, the Church said, should not be fast days, so the forty days stretched to an actual forty-six days, beginning with Ash Wednesday, the day after the festivities of Shrove Tuesday.

Many years ago, when people had committed serious sins, and had therefore been barred from taking communion in church (excommunication), they would wear their simplest clothes and scatter ashes on their heads as a sign that they were truly sorry. Then they would stand at the church doors and ask people to pray for them. Nowadays we sometimes say that a person is covered in 'sackcloth and ashes' when they are apologising for something they have done wrong.

Many people go to church on Ash Wednesday. In Roman Catholic churches, they file before the priest. He dips his thumb in ashes and makes the mark of a cross on their foreheads, saying to each person, 'Remember, man, that thou art dust, and unto dust thou shalt return.'

This service is still conducted in much the same way as it was a thousand years ago. The ashes are usually collected from palms used the year before on Palm Sunday; these are burnt, and the ashes placed on the altar and sprinkled with holy water.

In London a special service is held each year on Ash Wednesday in St Paul's Cathedral. It was first held when a man called John Norton, a member of the Worshipful Company of Stationers, died and left a sum of money to pay for the annual service.

The members of the Stationers Company still process in their velvet hats and fur-trimmed gowns to the Cathedral every Ash Wednesday.

In the old days, the period of Lent was very strictly observed. People gave up eating meat, butter, eggs, and other rich foods.

There is a record that King Edward III ordered vast quantities of fish for the royal household during the Lenten weeks. Many people still prefer to eat fish instead of meat during Lent.

Generally, Lent cannot have been a very pleasant period in those far-off days, and people must have longed for the time to pass quickly. Just as we now use Advent Calendars to mark off the days leading up to Christmas, so the people then made special 'calendars' to mark off the passing weeks of Lent.

In France and Greece, and some other countries, children still make traditional Lent Calendars as they did hundreds of years ago.

A GREEK KUKARAS (Lenten Calendar)

Make a calendar as the children do in Greece.

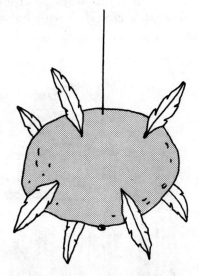

Take a fairly large potato and scrub it clean. Carefully pierce a hole right through it using a skewer or knitting needle. Thread a piece of string through the hole, making a knot in the end of it to secure the potato. Find seven large feathers (perhaps a butcher will give you some), and stick these into the potato, which should then be hung up by the string.

If you cannot find any feathers, make your own with paper and a cocktail stick, as shown. Pull out one feather at the end of the first week of Lent, and then one each week until Easter.

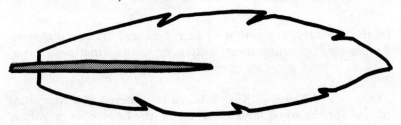

FRENCH PAPER 'NUNS' (Lenten Calendar)

These are still made by some French children to mark off the weeks of Lent.

Trace the nun shape onto card, then colour it and cut it out, being very careful when you cut round the seven feet!

Hang the 'nun' from a piece of string or thread. At the end of each week in Lent, tuck one of her feet under, until at Easter she has none at all!

MOTHERING SUNDAY

The people who, long ago, kept Lent so strictly, must have been glad to have a celebration half way through it. It became the custom for families to gather together in their parents' home on the fourth Sunday in Lent.

Exactly when the custom began, or why, we do not know. Some people believe that it began in pagan times when the people worshipped Cybele, the mother of all the other gods, at this time of year.

When Christianity came, the priests used to call people to worship in mid-Lent in their 'Mother Church', that is, the church where they had been brought up. Many young people worked away from home. They would be hired for a year at an October Hiring Fair, and half way through their contracted time, on the fourth Sunday in Lent, they were allowed a day off to go home. After a service in their Mother Church, it would be natural for them to go back to their mother's home for a meal and a celebration.

The young people always tried to take a gift for their mother: it might be a present of wild flowers picked on their way home, or a simnel cake made with ingredients supplied by their employers.

The word SIMNEL probably comes from the Latin word for fine white flour — *simila*. But there is also a legend about two young people from Shropshire who could have given their names to the cake.

Simon and Nell wanted to give their mother a cake, but could not agree how to cook it. Simon wanted to boil it, but Nell thought it should be baked. In the end they did both, and this type of cake became known as a SIM-NEL cake!

We do know, however, that the making of simnel cakes goes back a very long way indeed. They were being made even before the Norman Conquest!

Simnel cakes are still made today, although some people eat them at Easter instead of on Mothering Sunday. You may be able to find the recipe for one in a cookery book.

The real Shropshire simnel cake is still made as it was hundreds of years ago. It is full of rich ingredients, and is quite expensive to make. The main part is a normal fruit cake, similar to a Christmas cake, but the simnel cake has a crust made from flour and water wrapped round and over it. This crust is coloured yellow by adding saffron, and the whole cake, fruit mixture and crust, is wrapped in a cloth and boiled for several hours. Then it is brushed with egg and put into the oven to bake! By this time the crust is very hard indeed. Many old tales are told about people not knowing what to do with the cake they were given!

Nowadays many simnel cakes are made by putting half the fruit mixture into the cake tin, then a layer of marzipan or almond paste, and then the other half of the mixture. After being cooked, some are iced with marzipan and decorated with eleven marzipan eggs. It is thought that these eggs represented either the number of disciples present at the crucifixion of Jesus, or the number of months that the son or daughter had been away from the family home.

As well as these traditional cakes, other gifts were given to mothers on this particular Sunday. Some daughters made 'lambs tail biscuits', which were crisp biscuits flavoured with cinnamon and shaped to look like the tails of the new spring lambs.

Others made sugar plums with a hidden caraway seed or other sweet spice inside. Children brought posies of spring flowers: violets and primroses, gathered in the woods the day before or on their walk to their former home.

In various parts of the country other special foods were eaten. One was a dish called FURMETY or FRUMENTY. This was something like a sweet porridge made by boiling wheat grains in milk and adding sugar and sweet spices.

In Scotland soaked peas were fried in butter with pepper and salt and made into a kind of pancake. These were called CARLINGS. Mothering Sunday is still sometimes called Carling Sunday in Scotland.

45

① FLYING BIRDS

You will need:

   3 sheets of paper, about
     20 × 10.5 cm (or 8 × 4½ ins)
   Lengths of cotton
   Twig or small rod
   Colouring materials, scissors

Fold the pieces of paper in half.
Trace the bird below on to
the paper, putting its
back on the fold.
Cut out the bird

1. Fold forward, then back.

B

A

2. Open
shape, then
fold tail towards
head on this line

Fold
wings
up each
side of
body

Follow the instructions
for folding, then open bird flat and
press down at A. Squeeze parts
together

A

Make eyes by
punching holes, or
draw them with felt pens. Colour the
birds brightly. Attach cotton at B;
each bird should hang at a
different length from the twig.

(Pack carefully so as not to tangle the cotton)

② ROSE BUTTONHOLE

You will need:

Rose coloured crepe or tissue
paper, 30 x 7·5cm (or 12 x 3 ins)
Long knitting needle
Green paper
A postcard
Green wool, scissors, glue,
silver foil, thin wire.

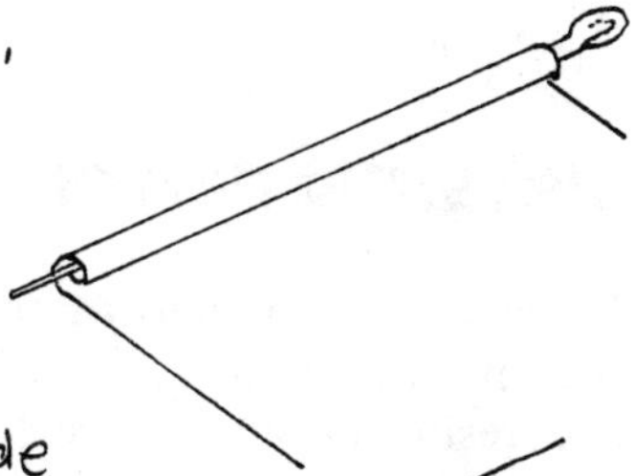

The Rose:

Lay the knitting needle
along the long side of the
rose paper, and roll it over
for about 2·5cm (or 1 in). Slide
out the knitting needle.

Now roll the paper as shown.
Tie at the base with wire,
leaving 2 long ends. Twist these
together and bind with green wool.

The leaf spray:

Cut out 5 leaves from the green paper,
using the pattern (right). Cut the
'stalk' from the postcard. Colour it
green with a felt-tip pen. Glue the
leaves on as shown.

Lay the rose on top of
the leaf spray. Wrap
both 'stalks' in
silver foil.

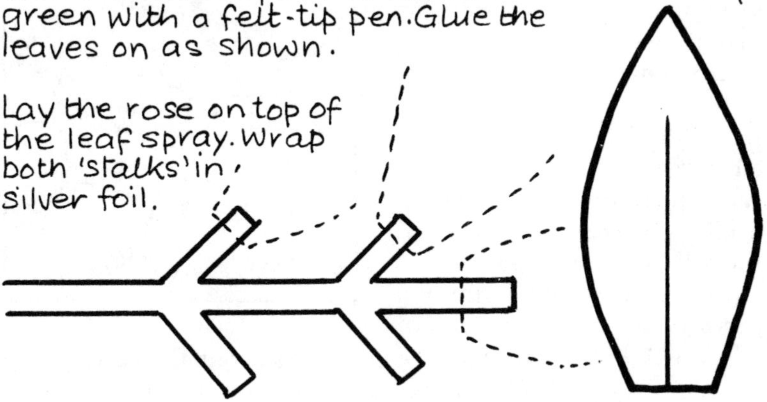

PASSIONTIDE

The last two weeks of Lent are called Passiontide, and the week beginning on Palm Sunday is called Holy Week. For Christians, Holy Week is the most solemn time in the whole year. During it people are remembering Christ's passion, the agony and suffering he went through before his death. Churches remind people of his suffering by having special services, plays or music during the week.

PASSION PLAYS

From very early days there have been passion plays, which were first performed to tell ordinary people the story of the death and resurrection of Jesus. Sometimes they were staged in the churches and sometimes in the streets so that more people could watch them. They were always very dramatic.

The Oberammergau Passion Play

A very special play is performed in the village of Oberammergau, in Bavaria. It is staged only once every ten years, but during the season one hundred performances are given. In some special years extra enactments of the play are put on. 1984 is the 350th anniversary of the beginning of the play, so many people will gather to see it performed in the 'extra' year.

In 1633 the village of Oberammergau found itself surrounded by an epidemic of a killing plague. Miraculously, the villagers were spared, and vowed they would write and perform a play as an act of thanksgiving to God. They decided to act out the suffering of Jesus in the days leading to his death and resurrection.

The play was written by a monk, and the music composed by the village schoolmaster. The people were ready for their first performance by 1634.

Everyone in Oberammergau was involved with this first play, and so they are even now, when people from all over the world travel to see it.

So many actors are anxious to take part in it that the authorities in the village decided to make some very strict rules. Only those, they said, who had been born in the village, or those who had lived there for twenty years, might be in it.

The Glorification of Christ – Oberammergau Passion Play.

All the villagers help in some way, even if they cannot have a part in the actual play. They run hotels for visitors; some make beautiful wood-carved souvenirs; others build stages and seating; and some arrange the musical accompaniments.

WOODCARVER AT WORK

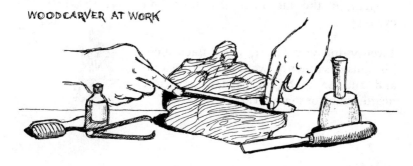

PASSIONTIDE MUSIC

Music always plays a big part in Holy Week. Apart from the special hymns sung in churches on Good Friday, a lot of music has been written to be performed particularly over the Easter season.

One of these pieces of music sung as an oratorio was written by Johann Sebastian Bach. He took the words from Matthew's Gospel account of the crucifixion and set them to music, calling it the *St Matthew Passion*. He supervised the first performance in Leipzig, Germany, on Good Friday 1729.

Bach, who was at the time a teacher in the Leipzig choir-school, could not find enough professional musicians to take part, so asked some of his students, and members of his own family, to make up the full number. In all he had 34 musicians and 36 singers for this first performance.

The *St Matthew Passion*, as it was first performed, lasted for three hours, and was spread over the three Good Friday services in the morning, afternoon and evening.

Twenty-one years later, when Bach died, his music suddenly went out of fashion and the *St Matthew Passion* was not heard again for many years.

Then Mendelssohn, another composer who became famous, discovered Bach's great oratorio and put on a performance of it in 1829, exactly one hundred years after it was written.

Today, Bach's *St Matthew Passion* is heard year after year at Passiontide in many towns and cities, in churches, cathedrals and village halls.

The tune of one of our great Good Friday hymns comes from this passiontide music: *O sacred Head, sore wounded.*

Bach used the same words in his oratorio, but they were originally written even earlier, in the seventeenth century.

Other well-known passiontide music is *The Crucifixion* by John Stainer and *Olivet to Calvary* by J.H. Maunder.

Olivet to Calvary is in two parts, and covers the period from Palm Sunday to the crucifixion. The first part includes the entry into Jerusalem, and the cleansing of the temple. Part Two opens with the Last Supper, is followed by the story of the trial of Jesus, and ends with the crucifixion.

One of our best-known Good Friday hymns, *There is a green hill far away*, was written by an Irish lady, Mrs C.F. Alexander, who lived during the reign of Queen Victoria. We are told that she used to drive in a carriage to do her shopping in the town of Derry. The old town was still surrounded by stone walls. Near these was a grass hill, which always made Mrs Alexander think of Calvary where the cross of Jesus was erected. (There is no mention of Calvary being on a hill in the Gospels, though.)

When Mrs Alexander wrote 'There is a green hill far away, without a city wall' she was using the word 'without' to mean 'outside'. In some hymn books it is written this way. Mrs Alexander also wrote the words of other well-known hymns, including *All things bright and beautiful* and *Once in royal David's city*.

THE PASSION FLOWER

This climbing plant with its interesting flowers was first discovered in South America about 400 years ago. Perhaps the Jesuit priests who settled there used it like a picture to illustrate the stories of Christ's suffering at the crucifixion.

Right in the centre, three parts remind us of the nails which held Jesus to the cross. Below them five more parts make us think of the five wounds he received. Round the centre a spiky circle stands for the crown of thorns. The ten petals stand for the ten disciples, excluding Judas who betrayed Jesus, and Peter who denied him. The flower's latin name is *Flos passionis*, the flower of the passion of Jesus. The plant also has delicious fruits.

PALM SUNDAY

We learn from the Bible that when Jesus entered Jerusalem near the time of the Passover Festival the people of the city went out to meet him with branches of palm trees, shouting,

'Praise God! God bless him who comes in the name of the Lord! God bless the King of Israel!' (John 12.13, GNB)

Palm Sunday marks the beginning of Holy Week, which leads up to the events of Easter. Christian churches all over the world keep this day to praise and welcome him.

Before the reformation of the Church in England in the sixteenth century, there were extremely elaborate ceremonies and celebrations on all the church festivals and feast days. Many of them were forbidden when the Protestant Church became the one to which people were expected to belong. King Henry VIII said, however, that he would allow the carrying of palms to be continued on Palm Sunday.

The climate here is not really suitable for many palm trees to grow as they do in hot Meditteranean countries. People, looking for an alternative, found that the furry grey-white flowers of the sallow willow were in bloom at this time of year, and gathered these instead. The tree quickly became known as the 'willow-palm'.

If you are unable to obtain palm, the crosses may be made quite effectively from long, thin strips of paper.

If you can use palm, first soak it and, while still damp, split in half lengthwise (1).

Place piece (b) across (a) using wide end of palm (2), take it behind (a) and back across in front of (a), wrapping tightly (3).

Make one arm of the cross by folding (b) across in front of (a), leaving the fold the required length.

Make the other arm by folding (b) back on itself, in front of (a), tucking the end between the right-hand fold to leave the second arm the same length as the first (4). It may be necessary to trim the end of (b).

Fold the short end of (a) down over (b) (5), then fold the long end of (a) up over its short end (6).

Turn it over so that the long ends point downwards and the small loop made by (b) is towards you (7).

Pass the long end of (a) up through the loop (8), pulling tight, and then down again leaving enough at the top to make the upright part of the cross (9). Trim end to required length.

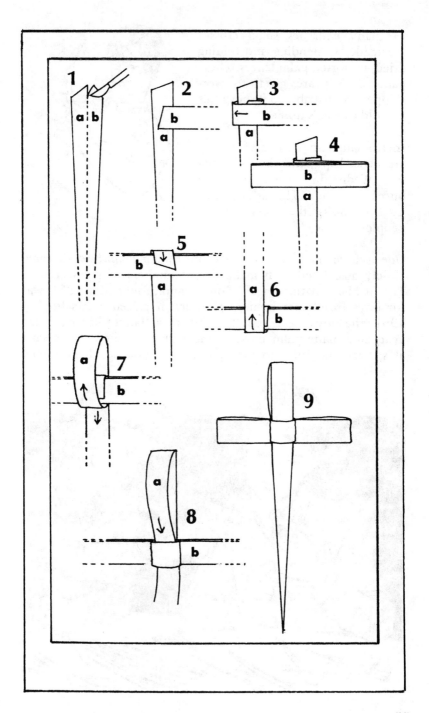

In many churches small crosses are made by bending and folding dried, imported palm leaves. These palm crosses are given to worshippers or distributed in hospitals and old people's homes.

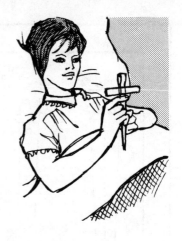

In Roman Catholic churches they are often kept until the following Ash Wednesday, when they are burnt to ashes. The ash is then used to make the cross sign on people's foreheads.

One school near Beaconsfield in Buckinghamshire became closely associated with making vast numbers of palm crosses. The St Mary of the Angels' Song School, founded in 1931, was for boys from poor homes. Although it closed as a school in 1961, the boys were kept together as a 'family home'. Every year they made palm crosses, and formed a choir which sang at special functions, to help pay for the upkeep of the home.

Every year in Jerusalem, Christians from all over the world meet to take part in a Palm Sunday procession along the very roads used by Jesus as he entered Jerusalem so long ago. They carry palms, and sing praises as they go.

In Italy, instead of carrying palm branches, the people pick boughs from the olive trees and wave these in the processions.

In some of the large cities in Spain, Mexico, and South America, there are big processions every evening of Holy Week. Huge statues, each needing dozens of men to carry them, are taken through the streets.

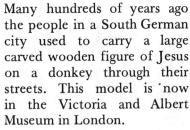

Many hundreds of years ago the people in a South German city used to carry a large carved wooden figure of Jesus on a donkey through their streets. This model is now in the Victoria and Albert Museum in London.

In other German cities it was quite common for the priests to ride on a donkey to their Palm Sunday services.

In Palestine, when Jesus was alive, most travellers used donkeys to get them from place to place. They are reliable and sure-footed animals, and are highly valued there.

In biblical times the Jewish people longed for a Messiah, a Saviour, to free them from the oppression of their enemies. They had been told by wise men for hundreds of years that he would come one day.

In the Old Testament, the book of the prophet Zechariah records:

'Rejoice, rejoice, people of Zion!
    Shout for joy, you people of Jerusalem!
    Look, your king is coming to you!
He comes triumphant and victorious,
    but humble and riding on a donkey —
    on a colt, the foal of a donkey.'   (Zechariah 9.9, GNB)

When a king came to his capital city 'triumphant and victorious', he rode on a war horse. Jesus chose to ride into Jerusalem on a humble donkey. But pilgrims coming for the Passover were expected to walk into the city, so Jesus was giving the people a 'picture message' in two parts. First, he was letting them know that he was coming as a king, by riding; and secondly, that he was showing them the kind of king he was — not a king connected with war and hate, but a king of peace and love.

A lovely legend connected with the donkey is that the cross of dark hair on its back only appeared after Jesus had ridden into Jerusalem on one.

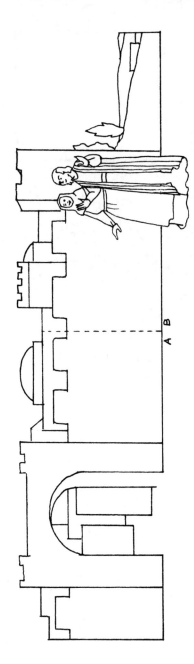

To make the frieze without spoiling the pages of this book you will need to trace the pieces onto white paper, colour them, and then cut them out.

Find a piece of coloured paper (yellow or pale blue would be best) as a background for the figures and the city walls.

Stick on the two sections of the 'walls' (A and B) first, fairly near the top of the background paper.

Next stick on the crowd figures in front of the city walls, overlapping them if necessary, arranging them as you like.

Lastly, attach the figure of Jesus and the donkey. To give the frieze a 3-D effect, first stick a piece of thick cardboard on the back of the donkey. When the glue is dry, paste the other side of the cardboard strip, and stick it onto the frieze.

59

Glue under A to join

B

MAUNDY THURSDAY

The word 'Maundy' means commandment. On the night of the last supper which Jesus shared with his friends, he said to them, 'And now I give you a new commandment: love one another. As I have loved you, so you must love one another.' (John 13.34, GNB). Earlier that evening, Jesus had washed his disciples' feet, to set them an example of service. It was later that evening when Jesus was arrested.

So on Maundy Thursday, the day before Good Friday, rich and famous people used to humble themselves, as Jesus had done: they became servants to the people who normally served them.

In the old days the King or Queen used to wash the feet of poor people, the number of poor people depending on how old the monarch was. When Queen Elizabeth I was 39, she was attended by 39 ladies of her court, and ordered that 39 needy people should be lined up in front of her. She then knelt and washed their feet, but only after they had been given a preliminary wash by the court ladies! The poor people were also given gifts of clothes and food in small baskets which were called 'maunds'.

The last King of England to wash the people's feet was James II. After that, a royal almoner was instructed to kneel and wash the feet on the monarch's behalf, and so gradually the custom died out. But the gifts were still distributed, with money being given, in small white leather bags, as well as food and clothes.

When Queen Victoria gave out the 'maunds' she still used specially minted money in white bags, but added more money in little red bags instead of the food and clothes.

Our Queen carries on this old tradition of giving Maundy money, usually at Westminster Abbey, but sometimes at other cathedrals.

She walks in procession to the Maundy Thursday service, then distributes the Maundy money to old people: one old man and one old woman for each year of her age. She is always presented with a posy of flowers and sweet herbs, a tradition which goes back to the time when sweet herbs were supposed to protect one from the plague!

In Germany, the Thursday before Good Friday is known as Green Thursday. The people who had confessed on Ash Wednesday were then given green branches as a sign that they had been truly forgiven. Now, on this day, children in Germany are given green eggs — hens' eggs that have been dyed in spinach water.

THE CROSS

Crucifixion was a particularly cruel method of execution for criminals in the days of Jesus. The condemned person had to carry his cross to the place of hanging, where he was stripped of his clothes. Imagine how the hot sun and the biting insects must have been an extra torture for the crucified person!

Cruci fixus were the Latin words meaning 'fixed to a cross', from which we get our word crucifixion. This form of killing first came from the Phoenicians, and was adopted by the Romans, who used it often. Sometimes many people were crucified at the same time. Roman citizens could not be killed in this way, even if they were the worst kind of criminal. It was a method used for slaves and servants, particularly those who rebelled against the State of Rome.

Have you noticed how many of our churches are built in the shape of a cross? In architecture, and in other connections, this is called a cruciform shape.

This little church in Sussex was built in a very simple cross shape nearly a thousand years ago.

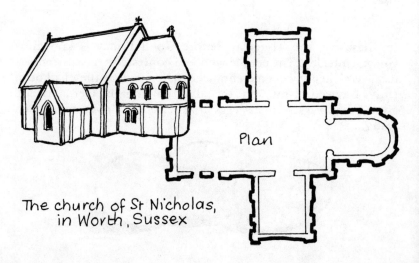

Plan

The church of St Nicholas, in Worth, Sussex

All these things are 'cruciform', although not necessarily anything to do with the cross of Jesus. Can you name them?

(Answers on page 128)

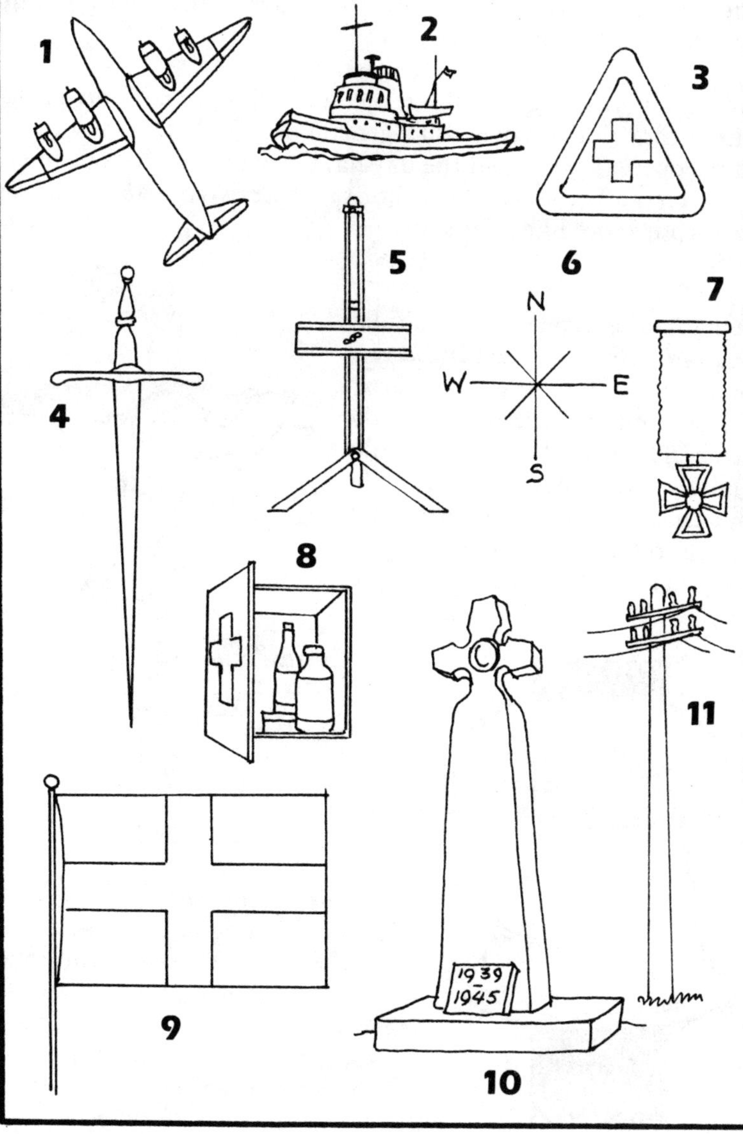

1

2

3

4

5

6

7

8

9

10

11

GOOD FRIDAY

Good Friday has been kept as a specially solemn day throughout the ages — a day when Christians in every country think of the death of Jesus. There are services in most churches, some of them held between 12 noon and 3 o'clock in the afternoon, the time when Jesus died.

Not many years ago all the shops were closed on Good Friday but, although the day is still a general holiday here, many of the shops open as usual, and the day has become very little different from any other day. The majority of Christians, however, try to keep it more like a Sunday.

Perhaps the name Good Friday was once God's Friday. In Eastern churches it is known as Great Friday, and in Germany it has the name Silent Friday — Der Stille Freitag. In that country the churches are silent, no bells ring, the church altars are bare, and the priests are dressed in black.

Crucifixion from a 13th century psalter

In some churches the 'Nine Tailors' is rung by the bells on Good Friday. The bells ring one note nine times, then there is silence before they are rung thirty-three times, one for each of the years Jesus lived.

Most people in this country think of hot cross buns when they plan for Good Friday. The custom of eating these goes back a long, long way. Even before the time of Jesus, the Greeks and Romans used to eat special small cakes during the early spring festival. When the Romans conquered Britain they brought the custom with them, and we know that, in Saxon times, small cakes made from wheat flour were eaten at this time of year.

When Christianity spread, the people of Britain continued to make and eat the little wheaten cakes, but added a cross to them to remind them of the way in which Christ died.

We have eaten hot cross buns of the type we know today since the early 18th century. Housewives used to be up early on Good Friday morning to make buns for the family.

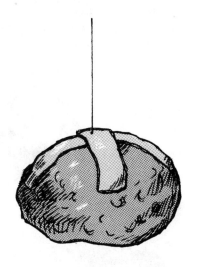

There was an old belief that a bun made on Good Friday morning would never go bad, and people used to keep one for months, or even for a whole year! If someone became ill, a bit of this bun was broken off and given to them. Perhaps it did them some good containing, as it must have done after all that time, a form of penicillin!

Sometimes a bun was hung from a kitchen ceiling, where it soon became hard and dry.

In East London a public house called *The Widow's Son* keeps up a strange Good Friday tradition. It stands where once a widow and her sailor son had their house. One Good Friday, expecting her son home from sea, the widow got up early to bake him a batch of buns. But he never arrived home to eat them. The widow refused to believe that he had been lost at sea, and that she would never see him again, and kept one of the buns for him.

When the next Good Friday came she baked more hot cross buns, and again kept one for him. And every year after that she made, and kept, a special bun for her sailor son.

Now, in the pub that stands where her house had been, the landlord keeps up this custom. A great many buns hang from the ceiling, some of them very old indeed, and each year a sailor is invited to add another one!

Some towns and villages keep up their own particular traditional celebrations on Good Friday.

In Bedfordshire, children gather each year on Dunstable Downs to roll oranges down a steep bank there. It is said that this rolling helps them to remember how the stone on Christ's tomb was rolled away. There are other rolling customs, too, which usually take place on Easter Monday. (See page 88.)

Playing marbles was a favourite holiday pastime in the old days, and a world-wide marbles championship is held every Good Friday in Tinsley Green, West Sussex.

This began, so the story goes, when two men wished to marry the same girl. Instead of the usual duel, they decided to settle the matter with a marbles match. They must have enjoyed it, because they met each succeeding year, inviting others to join in. We do not know whether either of them in fact married the girl!

Over the years the contest of marbles has grown until now the World Marbles Championship is held in the village each year.

Skipping, too, was an activity often connected with Good Friday. Both men and women skipped and, as on Shrove Tuesday, skipping contests and displays were common. Brighton is one of the places where skipping ropes can still be seen in plenty on Good Friday.

Over the years, children in and around Liverpool have found a good reason for making Good Friday into a kind of 'bonfire night'. This custom, known as the 'Burning of Judas', goes back to the days when Spanish ships sailed regularly into Liverpool Docks, bringing the custom with them. 'Punishing Judas' (the disciple who betrayed Jesus) was already a sport in many Mediterranean countries, and is still continued in some of them.

In Liverpool a few children still keep up the tradition, although now the authorities look upon the whole thing as a dangerous fire hazard. A model of Judas is made, rather like a Guy Fawkes, and the children go from house to house shouting, 'Judas is short of a penny for his breakfast!' If they are lucky they are given money and, later in the day, Judas is burnt on a bonfire.

Make your own Hot Cross Buns

These buns are made without yeast, so they are not true buns, but they are marked with a cross, which makes them special for Good Friday. They can be made very quickly.

For the buns

100g (or 4oz) margarine
100g (or 4oz) caster sugar
200g (or 8oz) self-raising
    flour
150g (or 6oz) sultanas
½ teaspoon mixed spice
pinch salt
a little milk

For the crosses

25g (or 1oz) magarine
50g (or 2oz) self-raising flour
1 dessertspoon water

(These ingredients will make about 10 buns)

Put all the dry ingredients for the buns into a bowl and mix with the milk until the mixture is smooth and firm. Form into small balls and put these, fairly wide apart, on a greased baking tray. Press them lightly with your fingers so that they are slightly flattened.

Mix all the ingredients for the crosses and knead for two minutes. Roll out on a floured board and cut into very thin strips. Cut these to about 5cm (or 2ins) long. Lay two pieces in the form of a cross on top of each uncooked bun.

Bake about 12 minutes in a hot oven (450°F, 225°C, Gas 7). The buns are delicious hot or cold when split in two and spread with butter.

EASTER SUNDAY

This is the happiest day of the year for Christians. After the solemn Holy Week, everyone rejoices that the dead Jesus became alive again. Church bells ring early on Easter morning, and the churches themselves are decorated with spring flowers. Nearly all churches hold a communion service on Easter Sunday.

All over the world, on this happy day, people greet each other with the words, 'Christ is risen!'

In some countries, where Christianity is frowned upon, words like these have to be whispered, or spoken only in the secrecy of the home, but everywhere true Christians can be spotted — by their look of gladness.

Make a list of all the joyful Easter hymns you sing or hear at Easter, in school, in church, or on the radio or television.

At sunrise on Easter morning Christians in the United States of America meet in some of the most unusual places for a service of praise and thanks. One of these is held on the rim of the Grand Canyon!

THE DATE OF EASTER

Easter is the most important Christian festival, and it is also the oldest. The fact that Jesus rose from the dead led to the basic Christian belief that after we die we live in Christ.

Easter Sunday is not always on the same date every year. Christmas Day is always on 25 December, but Easter Day can be on any Sunday between 21 March and 25 April. This does not mean that someone important looks at the calendar and says, 'April 6 seems to be a good Sunday to have Easter Day this year; we'll announce it to the world!' Easter IS a movable date from year to year, but its movement depends on the phases of the moon.

The Christian calendar, ie. the dates for festivals such as Christmas and Easter, grew out of two other calendars, the Jewish one, and the Roman.

The Jewish calendar depended on the moon and its phases; perhaps this was because the ancient Hebrews so often travelled by night. They even had a feast to celebrate the new moon. Read about something that happened during this feast, in 1 Samuel 20.5. The Jews counted their months by the waxing and waning of the moon.

The sun, however, was more important to the Romans, whose dates were fixed, and whose festivals took place on the same days each year.

When Christianity spread, the crucifixion of Jesus was deeply connected with the Jewish Feast of Unleavened Bread, or the Passover. At about the time when the Jews were sacrificing lambs for the Passover (these were called paschal lambs), Jesus was dying on the cross. By his followers, the new Christians, he was looked upon as the Lamb of God, sacrificed for men everywhere.

1983 April 3rd

1984 April 22nd

1985 April 7th

1986 March 30th

1987 April 19th

1988

So Easter became a festival with its date fixed by the Jewish lunar calendar. The Spring Equinox is 21 March, when the day and night are of equal length. Easter Day comes on the Sunday following the first full moon on, or after, the Spring Equinox.

Many other Christian festivals are decided by the date on which Easter Day falls, such as Ash Wednesday, Ascension Day, and Whitsun.

However, the date of Christmas was fixed on 25 December to replace a pagan Roman festival on the same day, the Feast of the Unconquered Sun.

By the Middle Ages, every day of the year had become some special feast or Saint's Day. When the Reformation of the Church in England came about, the Church calendar was re-formed and made simpler.

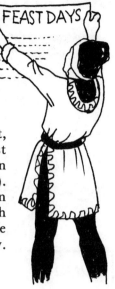

Only thirty-two days were now important, and these were all based upon the life of Christ or on some biblical saints, such as St Stephen (26 December) or St Andrew (30 November). The more important of these were printed in red, the less important ones in black, which gives us the phrase, 'A red-letter day'. Some diaries still have them printed in this way.

The name EASTER does not come from anything Christian or biblical. It was from the name EOSTRE, the pagan goddess of the spring!

Other countries, especially European ones, have names for Easter that are based on the Hebrew word PESACH, or PASSOVER.

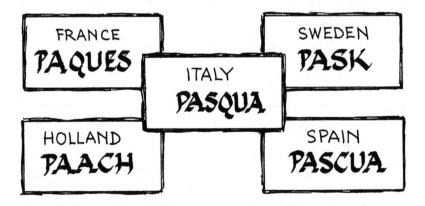

FRANCE
PAQUES

ITALY
PASQUA

SWEDEN
PASK

HOLLAND
PAACH

SPAIN
PASCUA

AN EASTER DIARY

For Simon Peter, the friend and follower of Jesus, the week which included Jesus' death must have seemed the worst of his whole life.

Pretend he had kept a diary each day. Write here a reminder of what probably happened every day.

Sunday	Mark 11. 1-11

Monday	Mark 11. 15-19

Tuesday	Mark 12. 41-44

Wednesday	Mark 14. 3-9

Thursday	Mark 14. 17-31, 53-54, 66-72

Friday	Mark 15. 21-39

Saturday	Matthew 27. 62-66

On the next day, Peter might have marked the diary with a huge star, because it was a wonderful day!

Write about it here:

Sunday   Luke 24. 1-12

EASTER EGGS

Even without Christianity and Easter itself, we should probably still hold a festival at this time of year, and eggs would probably play an important part in it. The excitement of returning spring makes people happy, and eggs are a symbol of new, returning life. They were often used in pagan festivals.

The first Christians used to take baskets of eggs to church to be blessed on Easter morning.

The first real Easter eggs were called PACE eggs, from the word PESACH, Passover. They were hard-boiled, dyed bright colours, and eaten for breakfast on Easter morning.

In those days, dyes were made at home from natural things like beetroot, onion skins, and spinach leaves. Material for clothes was also coloured with these dyes which were not permanent or 'fast', •as are the manufactured dyes of today. Little bits of coloured cloth were wrapped round the eggs when they were boiled, and the dye stained the eggshell.

Many families still colour their boiled eggs for Easter morning breakfast, adding food colouring to the water the eggs are boiled in. Some families boil the eggs in plain water, then use felt pens or paints to decorate the shells before the eggs are eaten.

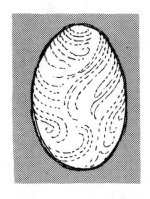

As time went on, artificial Easter eggs were made, carved in wood, or moulded in precious metals, cut from marble, or even wax; they were blown in glass, or carved in ivory. Not many of these old eggs have been kept, but the ones that survive are now sold for very large sums of money. They were originally given as special gifts at Easter time.

One of the Russian Tsars, Alexander III, ordered his court jeweller to make some expensive Easter eggs for his family.

Carl Fabergé, the jeweller, made them in gold, and decorated them with diamonds, pearls and emeralds. They were made so that they would open to reveal more priceless treasures inside.

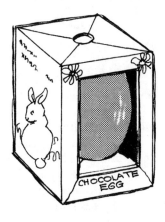

It became customary to make egg shapes in food such as marzipan or stiff icing. But it was only about one hundred and fifty years ago that the first chocolate eggs were made.

Now, Easter would not be the same without them. For weeks before Easter they are on sale in the shops, and are bought to be hidden away until Easter morning.

The first Easter eggs to be made after the discovery that hard-setting chocolate could be made from cocoa beans (until then people had used chocolate only as a drink) were made of solid chocolate, and were very sweet and rich.

In the 1920s the first hollow eggs were made by hand, by swirling melted chocolate round tin-plate moulds and leaving them to set. The two halves were then held together with satin ribbon, and the eggs, very large, were decorated with edible flowers and sprays of fern or lace. Sometimes they were filled with chocolates or sugared almonds.

Hollow eggs were also made of cardboard, usually with a painted design, and trimmed with lacy paper. Parents often filled these with small toys or sweets.

MAKE YOUR OWN PATTERNED EGGS

Use a raw egg, or one that has been hard-boiled. Draw a design on it with a wax crayon — be careful if you are using a raw egg! Boil some water, adding about 2 teaspoons food colouring and a little vinegar. Put the egg in and boil it for about 10 minutes. (If it is already hard-boiled, boil it for a few minutes only.) Rub the egg gently while it is still warm, to remove the wax. The pattern will then show up. Polish the egg with a little cooking oil.

BLOWING AND DECORATING EGGS

Take an ordinary hen's egg and make sure that it is clean and dry.

Use a strong darning needle to pierce a hole at one end of the egg.

Do the same at the other end, wriggling the needle to make this hole a little larger and to break the yolk inside.

Now have a bowl ready to catch the contents of the egg. Blow through the larger hole, and the yolk and white should trickle through the other hole into the bowl. The shell will be very fragile when it is empty.

Wash it again, and stand it in an egg-cup to dry.

When dry, paint the shell with bright patterns. Use poster paint if possible.

Or stick small gummed paper shapes on it in patterns; or even small seeds, bits of pasta or lentils.

When completely dry, varnish the eggshell. (You can buy aerosol cans of picture varnish, which is ideal for this.) Leave the egg in the egg-cup. Spray the top half. When dry, turn the shell upside down and do the other half. Use clear sticky tape to fix a length of cotton, wool or ribbon to the egg to hang it up.

EGG CUSTOMS AROUND THE WORLD

POLAND

Pysanki eggs: these are traditionally decorated eggs, with elaborate patterns scratched on them. Pysanki means to scratch.

Hard-boiled eggs are covered in coloured beeswax, and a design is scratched into the wax. Then the eggs are soaked in dye, and boiled again to loosen the beeswax. This is then wiped away, leaving the pattern.

Plough

The first egg is always decorated with a ploughshare design, to signify the beginning of farm work in the Spring.

NORTH AMERICA

In Georgia, USA, 20,000 coloured hard-boiled eggs are hidden in woods near Stone Mountain. Hundreds of children, all between 3 and 9 years old, go off to find them.

In North Carolina, for the past 160 years, children have enjoyed Easter egg 'fights'! They bang coloured hard-boiled eggs together to see which will break first.

GERMANY

In many parts of Germany children put out nests they have made of moss, hoping that the 'Easter Bunny' will find them and fill them with eggs.

ITALY

Many Italian parents hide painted eggs in the garden for their children to find. Sometimes the eggs have long strings attached to them. The children can then follow the strings to find the eggs.

GREECE

Eggs, coloured red, are carried on Easter Sunday. When two people meet the eggs are knocked together, and the people say 'Christ is Risen!'

FRANCE

Many French children believe that eggs are brought by the Easter bells, and are hidden under bushes or in the branches of trees.

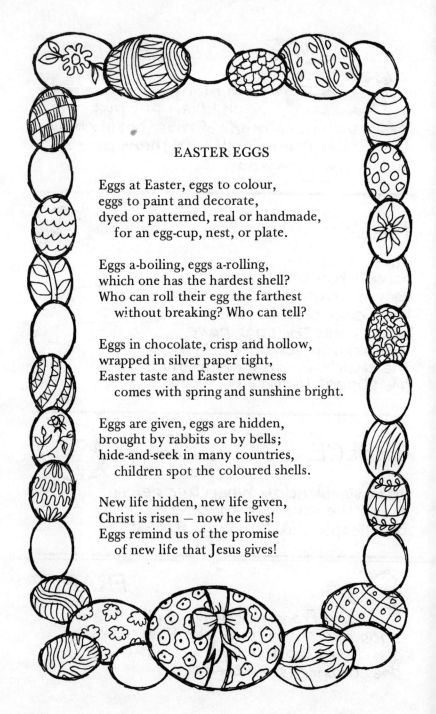

EASTER EGGS

Eggs at Easter, eggs to colour,
eggs to paint and decorate,
dyed or patterned, real or handmade,
   for an egg-cup, nest, or plate.

Eggs a-boiling, eggs a-rolling,
which one has the hardest shell?
Who can roll their egg the farthest
   without breaking? Who can tell?

Eggs in chocolate, crisp and hollow,
wrapped in silver paper tight,
Easter taste and Easter newness
   comes with spring and sunshine bright.

Eggs are given, eggs are hidden,
brought by rabbits or by bells;
hide-and-seek in many countries,
   children spot the coloured shells.

New life hidden, new life given,
Christ is risen — now he lives!
Eggs remind us of the promise
   of new life that Jesus gives!

EASTER MONDAY

For many years, the day after Easter Sunday has been a holiday, when shops, offices and banks are closed. It is a day of games and sports, and also for continuing many old customs connected with Easter. These vary from place to place, but many of them have something to do with the 'dole'.

Hundreds of years ago it was usual for rich people to leave some of their money, when they died, to be distributed annually amongst the poor, often at Easter time. This money was known as a 'dole'. Nowadays, the 'dole' is money given by the State to the unemployed.

Two of these 'dole' customs are still held annually, one in Biddenden, Kent, and the other in Hallaton, Leicestershire.

Long, long ago, two ladies of Biddenden left some land to the village people there, on the understanding that, every year, six hundred cakes were distributed from the window of a cottage on the land.

The two ladies, Elizabeth and Mary Chulkhurst, were Siamese twins, joined together at the shoulders and hips by ligaments. The village people looked after them well, and Elizabeth and Mary probably left them the land as a way of thanking them. The twins were born as long ago as 1100AD, and they died, within hours of each other, when they were 34 years old.

The Biddenden cakes, which are really more like biscuits, are still given out each year. They are made in the shape of the two ladies, and are imprinted with two numbers: 1100 and 34.

In Hallaton, in Leicestershire, some land was once left to the rector of the church there. In return for this 'dole' he had to provide a hare-pie, some bread and some ale, for which people 'scrambled'.

Nowadays a huge pie is still made, and baked in a large oven in a convent. It is then taken to the rector, who cuts it in pieces. These are taken to the top of a hill called Hare-Pie Bank, where the local people 'scramble' for them.

Later in the day another old custom takes place in the same village. Two teams of men compete in a long and often violent game played with kegs of beer. The course for the game is between two streams which are a mile apart. For anyone still able to dance afterwards, a ball is held in the evening.

These two customs are known as 'The Hare-Pie Scramble' and the 'Hallaton Bottle-Kicking Contest'.

There are many other strange old customs connected with Easter Monday in other parts of the country.

In Ossett, West Yorkshire, for instance, there is a coal-carrying contest each year. First the men carry a 50k (1cwt) bag of coal for about 1.7km (1 mile), going uphill all the way. Later the women have their own contest, but they carry only 12.5k (28lb) of solid fuel over a shorter course. There are money prizes and trophies for the winners.

One very old custom, followed in many different parts of the country, was 'Heaving' or 'Lifting'. It seems to have died out now — perhaps too many accidents resulted from it! On Easter Monday women sat on decorated chairs and were lifted high into the air by the men. This was repeated three times, or the chair was spun round three times while it was held aloft. The 'prizes' for this were hugs and kisses all round! The following day ladies gathered to 'lift' the men.

There is a record of King Edward I, in the 13th century, being 'lifted' by the ladies of the court, for which he had to pay them the sum of £14! Some people say that this custom began as a representation of the resurrection. It was supposed to bring good luck to all taking part.

Some of the old customs involve the use of eggs. In many places there are egg-rolling competitions still, where coloured, hard-boiled eggs are rolled, usually on grass, until the shells break. This is still done every year on the lawns of the White House, in the USA. Thousands of children are invited, and they compete to see who can roll their egg the furthest without cracking it. This custom has been going on there for about a hundred and fifty years.

In this country it used to be a good game to hold a hard-boiled egg in your clenched hand, and tap the end of it against an opponent's egg. It reminds us now of a game of conkers!

National games of football, and other sports, traditionally take place on Easter Monday.

Other countries, too, have their own events. In Sydney, Australia, there is an enormous agricultural show, called the Royal Easter Show. In it there are exhibitions of flowers, fruit and vegetables, cattle and sheep, and arts and crafts. There is also a big fun-fair and, in the evening, a firework display. In Australia, it is autumn when Easter comes, and growers and farmers spend their spring and summer preparing for the Show.

Try to find out if any old Easter customs still exist anywhere near where you live. Go and see them happen, if you can, and make sketches and notes, or take photographs; these may provide valuable historical records in the years to come, as many of the old traditions and customs are now dying out.

EASTER CUSTOMS IN BRITAIN

1. Skipping
2. Coal carrying
3. Burning of Judas
4. Coquille Buns
5. Hare-Pie Scramble
6. Pancake Race
7. Orange rolling
8. Biddenden Dole
9. Egg Shackling
10. Marble contest
11. Skipping
12. Westminster Greaze
    Stationers' service
    Widow's Son bun
        ceremony

1 Scarborough
2 Ossett
3 Liverpool
4 Norwich
5 Hallaton
6 Olney
7 Dunstable Downs
12 LONDON
Biddenden
9 Stoke St Gregory
8 Tinsley Green
10 Tinsley Green
11 Brighton

OPENING BUDS

Now is the time of year to notice flowers opening from their buds.

If you pick or buy a daffodil in tight bud, it will take only a day or two to open if you bring it indoors and stand it in water.

Notice how the petals gradually unfold, becoming bigger and stronger as they do so. You could make a drawing of it every day, to chart its progress.

HOW TO MAKE A PAPER 'FLOWER' OPEN OUT:

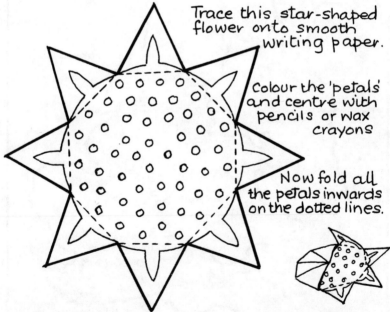

Trace this star-shaped flower onto smooth writing paper.

Colour the 'petals' and centre with pencils or wax crayons

Now fold all the petals inwards on the dotted lines.

Lay the 'flower' on a bowl of water and watch the petals open.

In April you may be able to find some beautiful madonna lilies (they have a Latin name too — *lilium candidum*) in the shops. They are often used to decorate churches at Easter.

You can buy tulips, too, which are strong and colourful.

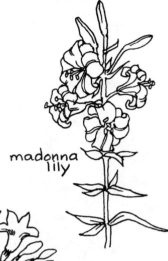

madonna lily

tulip

freesia

There should be freesias for sale; these have a lovely scent and come in many different colours.

Look out for magnolia trees, the flowers of which are large and whitish-pink. They usually bloom before there is any sign of leaves on the tree.

You may also see almond trees, with clouds of pink blossom, which scatters like confetti when the wind blows.

magnolia

almond

There are usually plenty of daffodils and narcissi in gardens in April.

Have you ever seen a wild daffodil? It is much smaller and narrower than our garden ones.

wild daffodil

celandine   primrose

violet

In the country you should be able to find primroses and celandine flowers growing and, if you look carefully, some tiny violets.

dandelion

Look, too, for dandelions along the roadside. They have lovely sun-like flowers; but do not pick them because they do not really like being brought indoors. Perhaps you will find a dandelion 'clock', a ball of light, feathery seeds.

small white butterfly

If there is some warm sunshine in April, you may see the first cabbage white butterflies flying about the garden looking for leaves on which to lay their single eggs.

HOW TO ENLARGE PICTURES

You can enlarge any of
the pictures in this
book using this method:

Trace the template or
picture and draw a
diagonal grid over
the tracing ➡

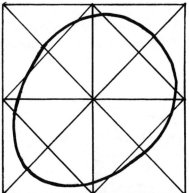

Make a similar grid
on the paper or card on which you want
to enlarge the drawing. (Make sure the
rectangular outline is in scale.) ➷

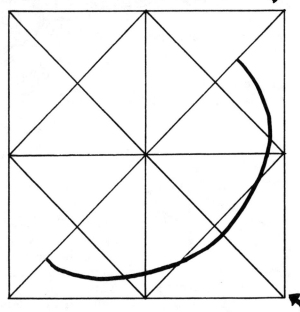

Enlarge the template one triangle at a time
until you have completed the picture.

EASTER TREES

Most of us have trees in our homes at Christmas time, but did you know that in many countries trees, or branches of trees, are a regular feature at Easter time?

Twigs and branches are cut and brought into the house a week or two before Easter so that they will be in bloom by Easter Day.

Other branches are put into deep flower pots and decorated with blown eggs or little wooden eggs. Many of these have been collected and are displayed in folk museums throughout the country.

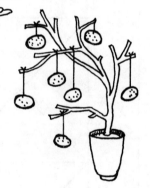

Children in Sweden also like to make 'Witch Trees'. These are branches of trees hung with little black paper witches riding on twig broomsticks. Sometimes Easter birds are hung between them.

HOLLAND

In Holland, families pick branches and spray them with gold or silver paint, and hang them with sweets and nuts.

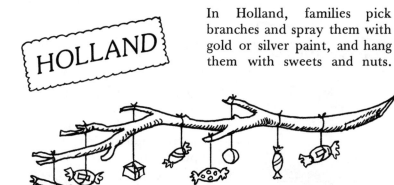

Dutch settlers took this custom with them long ago to America, and it is still carried on in many homes there.

GERMANY

Birch tree branches are often brought indoors and decorated with Easter eggs in German homes. Some families, however, choose a bush still growing in the garden, and hang this with eggs each year.

SWITZERLAND

Branches of flowering fruit trees are brought into Swiss homes and decorated with ribbons and painted blown eggs.

Children dance round the 'trees' making secret wishes, and are then invited by the adults to have cakes and coffee.

95

FRANCE

French children love to see branches of trees and bushes taken into their churches on Easter Sunday. The trees are put near the font and hung with flowers, eggs and ribbons.

MAKE AN EASTER TREE

Ask if you may pick a few budding branches from a tree. Plant them in a large flowerpot filled with earth or sand.

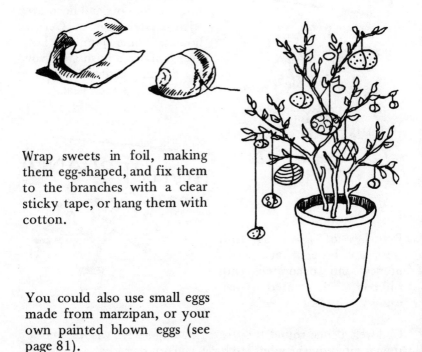

Wrap sweets in foil, making them egg-shaped, and fix them to the branches with a clear sticky tape, or hang them with cotton.

You could also use small eggs made from marzipan, or your own painted blown eggs (see page 81).

SPECIAL EASTER FOOD

Many countries have special traditional food that is eaten at Easter. In some countries, lamb is a favourite, probably in memory of the paschal lamb sacrificed at the Feast of the Passover. Among Christians, Jesus was thought of as the Paschal Lamb. The lamb is also a symbol of innocence. These words from the book of Isaiah in the Bible remind us of this:

'He was treated harshly, but endured it humbly;
   he never said a word.
Like a lamb about to be slaughtered,
like a sheep about to be sheared,
   he never said a word.
He was arrested and sentenced and led off to die,
   and no one cared about his fate.'

(Part of Isaiah 53. 7-8, GNB)

In this country we often eat fish on Good Friday, and chicken or turkey on Easter Sunday. Other countries have their own dishes.

ITALY

Panettone is a kind of cake or bread baked particularly at Easter or Christmas. Each loaf is decorated with sweet spice and sugar crystals, and has sugared lemon peel in it.

Dove cakes are often made at Easter, too. There is a story about a king who wanted to overthrow a city, but his horse refused to take him into battle. Only when a girl offered the horse a dove cake did it agree to move, but by then the king had changed his mind, thinking of the dove of peace. This is also called Colomba cake.

RUSSIA

In Russia a cake made with yeast is served. It is called Kulich. First the Kulich is taken to church for a priest's blessing, and later eaten with spiced cottage cheese.

POLAND

In Poland and other parts of Eastern Europe food is also taken to church, carried in baskets and covered with white cloths. Fruit and nut cakes are made in the shape of the crown of thorns. Polish children love to eat little 'paschal lambs' made in butter icing.

SICILY

There is a delicious sweet eaten by Sicilians at Easter time — layers of cake and ice cream, all covered in chocolate icing!

EAST AFRICA

'Matoke' is a favourite dish made by boiling unripe bananas with salt and pepper. These are usually served on a plate made of large banana leaves.

Further inland where fish is scarce, an Easter treat would be to eat some small dagaa fish, rather like sprats. Chicken (kuku) is also eaten, always boiled, and in a stew with tomatoes.

AUSTRALIA

Easter Sunday in Australia is a day when families try to be together. It is late summer in April, and usually warm and sunny. Many families spend the day on the beach or in the country, enjoying picnics or barbecues. Salads, cold chicken, and sausages are favourite foods.

99

EASTER CARDS TO MAKE

CARD 1

You need:

1 piece of white card about 20cm × 15cm (or 8½in × 5in)

1 piece of paper for the 'chick', about 10·5cm square (or 4in square)

Scissors, glue, crayons, felt-tip pens, or paint

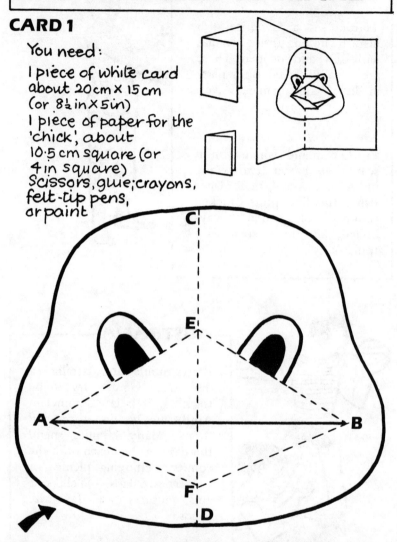

Trace this shape onto the smaller piece of paper, and cut out. Colour the chick's head yellow, leaving the eyes black and white. Colour the beak (AEBF) bright orange.

Slit A-B. Fold head inwards on C-D. Fold up on A-E and F-B, fold down on A-F and F-B.

100

The chick's head should now look like this:

Turn it over and glue all over the back of the head, but DO NOT glue the back of the beak.

Fold the white card in half.

Lay the chick's head in the centre of the white card, making sure that the fold, C-D, is on the centre fold of the card.
    Stick in place.

When dry, open chick's beak, and write 'From_____'(your name) on the white card showing inside.
On the front of the card write 'A HAPPY EASTER! (You could trace the letters below and colour them.) Make sure the beak stays OPEN when you close the card.

A HAPPY EASTER

CARD 2

You need:

A piece of thick paper about 25 cm x 10 cm (or 9 in x 4 in). Fold as shown. Scissors, colouring materials

Position of egg on card

Trace this egg shape on to the folded paper, making sure the edge of the egg (A-B) is on the fold of the card.

Cut out, except between A and B.

Trace the jagged 'hole' onto the egg shape, and cut out the shaded part (on the FRONT of the card only). Draw in the crack marks with felt-tip pen.

Write on the word 'GREETINGS' as shown.

Open out the card, and on the INSIDE trace
or copy the chick below, and colour it
bright yellow. (Leave the eyes black and
white.) The beak should be coloured orange.
Colour all the background a very dark
shade, like black or brown. When dry,
draw round the chick with black felt-
tip pen.

When you close the card the chick will
look through the hole!

Write your own
Easter message on
the back of the card.

Here are two Easter cards for you to trace, colour and cut out. Mount them on folded pieces of paper and write a message inside.

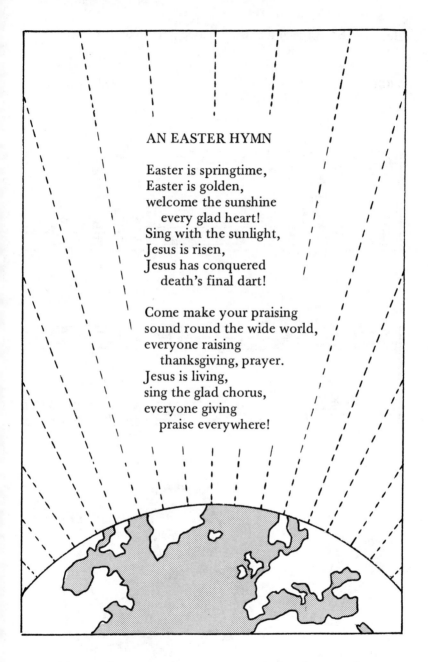

AN EASTER HYMN

Easter is springtime,
Easter is golden,
welcome the sunshine
    every glad heart!
Sing with the sunlight,
Jesus is risen,
Jesus has conquered
    death's final dart!

Come make your praising
sound round the wide world,
everyone raising
    thanksgiving, prayer.
Jesus is living,
sing the glad chorus,
everyone giving
    praise everywhere!

This new hymn can be sung to *Bunessan*, the tune for
Morning has broken.

105

Here are the words and music for two new songs for Easter.

MICHAEL

Roy Chapman © 1983

EASTER PRAISE

Come with your shouts of joy,
   On this Easter Day!
Bring your excitement here
   as you pause and pray.

All round you life begins:
   see the signs of Spring!
Think of your risen Lord,
   and your praises sing!

Dance if you want to, clap,
   or look up and pray,
this is the time to cheer,
   for it's Easter Day!

Now give glad thanks to God
   for the joy he gives;
Easter has come again,
   Jesus lives, he lives!

R.S. Tayler, © NCEC 1983

EASTER CAROL

Once more the countryside's alive
  with newly wakened Spring;
We'll dance to thank the living Lord,
    and crown him King!

The trees are showing buds of green,
  the sky is brighter blue;
we'll dance with joy to thank the Lord,
    and praise him too!

Once sleeping flowers are now in bloom,
  the sun will warmer be;
we'll dance to thank the Lord, for all
    our eyes can see!

But more than Spring makes us rejoice
  to be alive today;
we'll dance for Jesus, risen Lord,
    this Easter Day!

EASTER DECORATIONS

1. TABLE CENTRE

You will need:

A piece of tree bark
1 large and 1 small
  wrapped Easter egg
A deep bottle cap,
  covered in coloured silver paper (save sweet
  and chocolate wrappers and use them)
Some flowers with short stems
Modelling clay

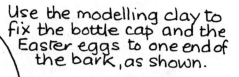

Use the modelling clay to
fix the bottle cap and the
Easter eggs to one end of
the bark, as shown.

Put water in
the bottle cap.

Fill the bottle cap with flowers, letting
them drape over the eggs and bark.

2. UNUSUAL DISPLAY FOR A
FORGOTTEN CORNER

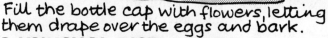

You will need:

A bunch of narcissus, tulips,
  or other flowers with strong stems.
An 'oasis' ball
A piece of dowel rod or bamboo, or
  a strong knitting needle
Yoghurt pot or cream carton
Sand or earth; ribbon; large paper
  doily; an elastic band

('Oasis' is a light, spongy material which, when soaked, holds water for a long time. It can be bought cheaply from flower shops. Ask for a ball-shaped piece.)

Soak the 'oasis' ball in water for at least an hour before using it for the display.

Fill the yoghurt pot with soil or sand, pushing it down well, so that the filled pot is heavy. Place the pot in the centre of a doily and pull the doily up round the pot. Fix it in place with an elastic band.

Cut the flower heads, leaving about 5cm (or 2in) of stem, and push the stems into the 'oasis' ball, until it is almost covered with flowers.

Leave a small area clear at the bottom of the ball. Push the rod firmly into the ball in the empty space.

Now push the end of the rod down into the sand in the yoghurt pot, packing it round so that it will stand upright.

Tie a piece of bright ribbon round the rod just under the ball of flowers.

AN ISLAND CALLED EASTER

They had sailed for weeks across the biggest ocean in the world, adventuring into the unknown. Captain Jakob Roggeveen, from Holland, with his two ships full of Dutch sailors, longed for the sight of land.

It was Easter Sunday in the year 1722, and the captain had tried to celebrate this holy day on board, but his shipmates were restless and beginning to wish they were at home with their families.

After lunch one of them gave a sudden shout, 'Land ahoy!' Captain Roggeveen looked in the direction the sailor was pointing, and tried to make out the faint shadow on the horizon.

He looked at his sea charts. No island was shown anywhere near where his ships lay. Had he sailed widely off course? Perhaps he was nearer to the great continent of America than he had imagined. He would sail nearer, to explore.

The shadow on the horizon darkened as the ships sailed closer. Captain Roggeveen could at last see high cliffs and the rocky coastline of an island. High on the cliffs puffs of smoke arose. The sailors rushed excitedly about the decks.

'The island is inhabited!' the word went round. 'People there have seen us! Those are smoke signals!'

The captain ordered the anchor to be dropped in the deep water away from the land, and waited. If he took the ships any nearer they would be dashed on the rocks, and they might never be able to get away.

He scanned the rocky headland. What he saw there made him start back in surprise and, at first, fear. Were the people of the island giants? Perhaps it would be safer to leave at once! But what he had at first taken to be figures of men standing in rows on the cliffs did not move and, as the mists cleared a little, Captain Roggeveen realised that they were not alive at all. They were statues, huge grey figures standing like sentries defending their coastline, most of them crowned with huge cylinders of some brownish stone.

The natives themselves, he could see now, were normal in size, and were scuttling between the statues and climbing down the gullies in the cliffs. Soon he could see men in one of the dark coves putting out to sea in narrow canoes.

'Welcome them!' ordered the captain, and his sailors lowered ropes so that the islanders could climb aboard. Everyone was surprised by their appearance. They were as fair-skinned as the natives of Tahiti, some with black hair and others with lighter, brown hair. Only a few were dark-skinned, making the captain think that perhaps they were a mixed race of people. He was struck by their elongated ears; many of them wore pegs like huge corks where European men sometimes wore ear-rings. The weight of these had made their ear-lobes dangle to their shoulders!

They seemed friendly enough, cheerful, peaceable, and with good manners, Captain Roggeveen wrote in his ship's log. Later, he was to find that they were also very accomplished thieves!

113

As darkness fell that Easter Sunday night, the natives took to their long, leaking canoes and paddled back to land.

'Tomorrow we will go ashore,' the captain promised his sailors.

At first light parties of men were put ashore and scaled the cliffs. What they saw astonished them: men, mostly naked but tattooed with rich patterns of birds and strange figures, squatted in a position of humble prayer, worshipping the sunrise.

Captain Roggeveen and his men were allowed to go close to the great statues. Some were as big as houses, others only twice as big as the men themselves. The Europeans had never seen anything like them before. They did not seem to have any bodies, but emerged from the earth at the shoulder-line, so that the heads were all tremendous in height. The captain tapped and prodded them. He could not imagine how they could possibly have been carved from heavy stone and then pulled upright. It would need remarkable engineering skills to be able to do that. He declared that they must have been modelled from a kind of clay, then, when they had been erected, filled with small stones to make them solid.

There seemed to be no women or children about, and the men appeared to have no weapons. No animals could be seen, except a kind of chicken strutting among the long, low reed huts.

Captain Roggeveen used hand signs to ask one of the men, 'What do you grow?' He was shown bananas, sugar cane, and fields of sweet potatoes.

The native men showed him their cooking 'stoves', red-hot stones sunken in the earth, on which were balanced earthenware pots of food. There seemed to be no metals on the island.

It seems surprising that Captain Roggeveen left this fascinating, unknown island on the evening of that first day. But perhaps he had seen all he wished to see. With friendly farewells, the natives let him go. It was only after the ships had put to sea again that the sailors found their hats had been stolen, and that the captain's best tablecloth was missing!

As Captain Roggeveen went to write about this day's adventure in his log book, he realised he did not even know the island's name. He thought back to his first sight of it, on Easter Sunday afternoon.

'It shall be known as Easter Island,' he wrote.

Find Easter Island in an atlas. It is still the loneliest inhabited place on earth, with a visit only once a year by a warship bringing supplies from Chile.

What has happened to the people of Easter Island and those statues examined by Captain Roggeveen since that day in 1722? There are many exciting books to read that will tell you. Find some in your library; they will continue the story for you.

IN THE COUNTRY
SEASONAL SPOTTING

Give yourself points for the things on this page that you can spot on country walks. (You could trace and colour the pictures, too.)

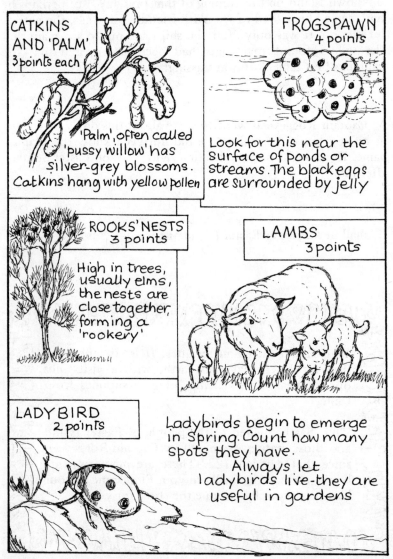

CATKINS AND 'PALM'
3 points each

'Palm', often called 'pussy willow' has silver-grey blossoms. Catkins hang with yellow pollen

FROGSPAWN
4 points

Look for this near the surface of ponds or streams. The black eggs are surrounded by jelly

ROOKS' NESTS
3 points

High in trees, usually elms, the nests are close together, forming a 'rookery'

LAMBS
3 points

LADYBIRD
2 points

Ladybirds begin to emerge in spring. Count how many spots they have.
Always let ladybirds live-they are useful in gardens

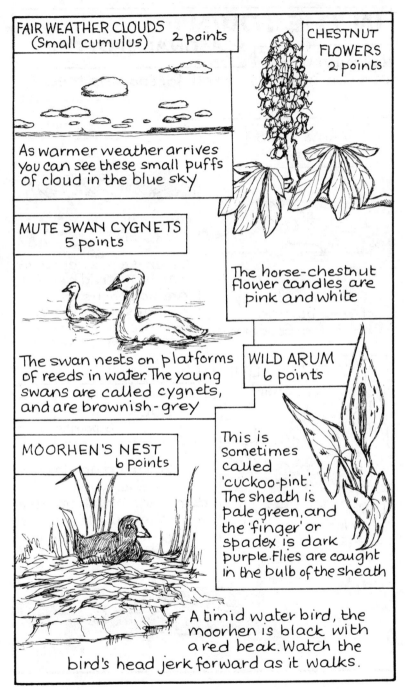

FAIR WEATHER CLOUDS
(Small cumulus)   2 points

As warmer weather arrives you can see these small puffs of cloud in the blue sky

CHESTNUT FLOWERS
2 points

The horse-chestnut flower candles are pink and white

MUTE SWAN CYGNETS
5 points

The swan nests on platforms of reeds in water. The young swans are called cygnets, and are brownish-grey

WILD ARUM
6 points

This is sometimes called 'cuckoo-pint'. The sheath is pale green, and the 'finger' or spadex is dark purple. Flies are caught in the bulb of the sheath

MOORHEN'S NEST
6 points

A timid water bird, the moorhen is black with a red beak. Watch the bird's head jerk forward as it walks.

117

IN THE TOWN

SEASONAL SPOTTING

How many points can you award yourself for spotting these?

HOT CROSS BUNS
3 points

You can usually buy hot cross buns a long time before Good Friday

YEW TREES
4 points

Often seen in church-yards. The red berries are poisonous to humans and animals. Branches are some-times used to represent 'palm' on Palm Sunday.

WASTE LAND LIVING AGAIN 3points

Look for plants and wild life in derelict areas

DUCKLINGS
6 points

The Mallard duck lays many eggs. When the ducklings hatch from the eggs they are led to the water and can swim immediately.

PUBLICITY FOR EASTER MUSIC OR PLAYS   4 points

TOWN HALL
ST MATTHEW
PASSION
-BACH-
FRIDAY APRIL 6th
7pm
THE CHOIRS OF
ST. PETERS
AND ST. ANNE'S
ORCHESTRA OF
RICHMOND
HIGH SCHOOL

Can you find notices for Easter plays or music on the radio or television?

DAISIES   3 points

Daisies begin to flower soon after Christmas. The petals are often pink-tipped

HOUSE MARTIN'S NEST   8 points

Built of mud under the eaves of houses, the nests are cup-shaped. The birds are white underneath.

COCKSFOOT GRASS   5 points

This is a coarse grass, often growing on waste places. The 'flowers' are green or purple, turning brown as the grass dries. The leaves are sharply pointed.

OTHER SPRING FESTIVALS

JEWISH

The Jewish Feast of PASSOVER is held in the Spring, near Easter time. It lasts for eight days and is sometimes called PESACH, or the Feast of Unleavened Bread.

At this time Jewish people remember when their ancestors escaped from slavery in Egypt to settle eventually in the Promised Land. They were instructed to bake unleavened bread (bread made without yeast) which could be made quickly as soon as their leader Moses gave the signal for them to leave.

Today, the Jews still eat only unleavened bread at Passover time. The special Passover meal is very much a family feast when foods which have a particular meaning are eaten: lamb, a symbol of the lamb sacrificed in the temple; roast eggs for new life; and bitter herbs to recall the bitterness of the people in slavery.

During the meal the youngest child always asks his father questions, and the answers to these tell again the story of how the Jews escaped from Egypt.

MUSLIM

Around the end of February the followers of the religion called Islam celebrate their prophet Muhammad's birthday. He was born just over 1400 years ago, and this is an important day for Muslims, who spend it in feasting and dancing.

HINDU

The Hindu festival of HOLI is a celebration for the arrival of Spring. It is a time when Hindus remember particularly how the god Krishna appeared, singing and playing the flute, and about his love for a girl named Radha.

New clothes are bought for the festival, and people love to spray each other with red powder and coloured water. In some places large statues of the gods are carried in procession round the streets.

SIKH

Early in April the Sikh people celebrate BAISAKHA. This recalls the day when the first Khalso ceremony was performed, baptising five men into the Sikh religion. It is the first day of the Sikh New Year.

Everyone goes to their place of worship, called a Gudwara, for prayers and hymns and readings from the Sikh Holy Book, the Guru Granth Sahib.

BUDDHIST

A Buddhist flower festival is held in the spring-time and the people decorate their temples with flowers, sprinkling scented tea around them. It is a time of happiness and rejoicing, of colour and music.

JAPANESE

In March the Japanese Girls' Doll Festival, or HINA MATSURI, is held. It is a very old celebration, and dolls have been handed down from mother to daughter over hundreds of years. The dolls are put on show for a week. At the end of the festival, children make paper dolls which they put in straw baskets and float off on the rivers. An old tradition says that the dolls will float off to another world.

CHINESE

In late January or February comes the Lunar New Year, a Spring festival for all Chinese people. It is a time for clearing up and cleaning, and for making the household gods happy. There is a national holiday, and families re-gather for a special meal.

One of their favourite foods at this time is jiaozi (pronounced jow-tsa): little pastry packets of minced pork, ginger and garlic. After the meal, everyone goes to visit friends and neighbours to drink tea. Often fire-crackers are let off, which used to be thought to frighten away evil spirits.

Two weeks later is the Lantern Festival. Again fireworks are lit, to encourage rain to fall, but the main celebration is one of lanterns, in the shape of fish or birds, or just large coloured globes, all lit by candles.

RUSSIAN

Easter is not an official time in Communist Russia, but Christians there observe it privately. The State, though, allows a special festival to mark the ending of winter, and this is similar to our Shrove Tuesday.

As with many of the spring festivals, MASLENNITSA began in pagan times. The word comes from the Russian word Maslo, meaning butter.

On this day the people dress up like gypsies, or sometimes as bears, and go from house to house collecting money. There is still plenty of snow about, so there are sleigh rides and snowball fights. Large, beautiful models are made in ice. There are fairs, carnivals, processions and dances. After dark, straw effigies representing winter are burnt.

Special pancakes called Blinis are cooked, and buns shaped like rings, called Bubliks, are eaten.

March 8 is Women's Day in Russia; it is a general holiday, when women are honoured with presents and cards, and awards for special services to the State are given.

SYRIAN

In Syria the Spring comes very quickly, the flowers blooming suddenly even in the desert places. At this time the people of Syria spend days feasting and drinking, and most of them camp out in the fields and on the hills.

EASTER PUZZLE PAGES

A TEASER

All the missing words in this story can be made using letters from the word EASTER. Can you work out what they are?

It was getting dark when Gary found a _ _ _ _ in the park. He began to _ _ _ _ _ _ at a _ _ _ _ in the night sky. 'It looks very bright through the branches of that _ _ _ _ _ ,' he thought. A friend came and _ _ _ _ next to him and started to _ _ _ _ _ him. 'You have a _ _ _ _ _ in your coat,' he said. Gary looked down, then realised it had been a joke. 'Come on,' he said. 'Let's go and have a cup of _ _ _ _ .'

CODED MESSAGES

The disciples of Jesus, when they entered Jerusalem on what we now call Palm Sunday, were aware that Jesus was wanted by the authorities, who were threatening to kill him. Early on the Friday morning of that week they may have wanted to get in touch with other friends of his, but it may have been dangerous to send normal messages. Here is one they might have written — in code. Can you work out what it says? (1 = B, 2 = C, and so on)

9.4.18.20.18.   26.17.17.4.18.19.4.3!
7.4.   8.18   8.13
6.17.4.26.19.   3.26.13.6.4.17!

On Easter morning the message would have been very different. Using the same code, write this message in numbers:

JESUS IS RISEN!

HE HAS BEEN SEEN!

Answers on page 128.

124

SPECIAL DAYS

Rearrange the letters in these words to make the names of special days connected with Easter time.

1   A SANDY PLUM
2   SEND A DYE WASH!
3   DOG FOR I DAY
4   ON HIS GERMAN DUTY

5   DEAR YEATS
6   NEED A STORY, MA?
7   US VETS RODE HAY
8   A CANDY PEAK

WHAT IS IT?

The first line of a well-known Easter hymn is hidden here. Decide which bits of words go together, and you will soon find the answer.

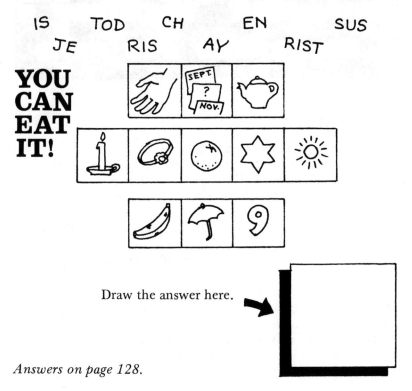

IS   TOD   CH   EN   SUS
JE   RIS   AY   RIST

YOU CAN EAT IT!

Draw the answer here. ➡

Answers on page 128.

EASTER CROSSWORD

Clues across
1   Scottish name for Mothering Sunday
2   Custom of raising people on chairs on Easter Monday
7   Hare-Pie _____ is held each year in Hallaton
8   On Maundy Thursday we remember how Jesus _____ the disciples' feet
10 There is an Easter service at this time of day at the Grand Canyon, USA
12 Name of a kind of sweet porridge served on Mothering Sunday in olden days
14 Waved when Jesus entered Jerusalem
16 Money left to be distributed by the rich
19 Maundy _____
20 and 5 down   Day after Shrove Tuesday
21 To 'shackle' an egg it must be this
23 The happiest day of the year for Christians

25 Mardi ___
26 Another name for 2 across
29 Where the pancake race is held in Buckinghamshire
32 This means a command
33 Goddess of the Spring in ancient times
34 You cook a pancake in this
35 Honour your mother on this Sunday
38 The date of Easter is based on the Jewish ___
39 Most Easter eggs nowadays are made of this
40 Consume
41 The first real Easter eggs were called ___ eggs

Clues down
1 Tradition
3 In Lent many people ___ , going without food
4 Some 31 down cakes are ___ with marzipan
5 See 20 across
6 These are eaten on Shrove Tuesday
9 The ___ of Easter is fixed by the moon's phases
11 Composer who wrote the St Matthew Passion
13 Unleavened bread is made without using this
15 On the day before Ash Wednesday, people were called to the church to be ___
17 Old English word for Spring, from which we get the word Lent
18 Men are required to carry a ___ of coal on Easter Monday in Ossett, Yorkshire
19 In Biddenden the Siamese ___ are remembered
22 Old Hebrew word meaning Passover
24 In many places egg ___ is a favourite pastime on Easter Monday
27 Jesus rode one
28 Westminster School has a Pancake ___ every year
30 Hot cross ___
31 Cake for Mothering Sunday or Easter
33 Perhaps you will have a chocolate one for Easter
34 Some early Easter eggs sell for a great
36 The Olney Pancake ___ is held every year
37 Legend says that Simon and this girl gave their names to a cake

Answers on page 128.

Cruciform shapes (page 65)   1 Aeroplane, 2 Radio mast on ship, 3 Cross-roads sign, 4 Sword, 5 Artist's easel, 6 Compass points, 7 Medal, 8 Red cross on medical cabinet, 9 Cross on flag, 10 War memorial, 11 Telegraph pole

A teaser (page 124)   Seat, stare, star, tree, sat, tease, tear, tea

Coded messages (page 124)   Jesus arrested! He is in great danger!
9.4.18.20.18 8.18   17.8.18.4.13!   7.4 7.26.18 1.4.4.13 18.4.4.13!

Special days (page 125)   1 Palm Sunday, 2 Ash Wednesday, 3 Good Friday, 4 Mothering Sunday, 5 Easter Day, 6 Easter Monday, 7 Shrove Tuesday, 8 Pancake Day

What is it? (page 125)   Jesus Christ is risen today

You can eat it (page 125)   Hot cross bun

Easter crossword (page 126)
Across: 1 Carling, 2 Lifting, 7 Scramble, 8 Washed, 10 Dawn, 13 Frumenty, 14 Palms, 16 Dole, 19 Thursday, 20 and 5 Down Ash Wednesday, 21 Raw, 23 Easter, 25 Gras, 26 Heaving, 29 Olney, 32 Maund, 33 Eostre, 34 Pan, 35 Mothering, 38 Calendar, 39 Chocolate, 40 Eat, 41 Pace
Down: 1 Custom, 3 Fasted, 4 Iced, 5 see 20 across, 6 Pancakes, 9 Date, 11 Bach, 13 Yeast, 15 Shriven, 17 Lengten, 18 Sack, 19 Twins, 22 Pesach, 24 Rolling, 27 Ass, 28 Greaze, 30 Buns, 31 Simnel, 33 Egg, 34 Price, 36 Race, 37 Nell